813.609 ERZ
Fanpire : the Twilight
saga and the women who lo
Erzen, Tanya.
960036

MT JAN 2013
B 2014
2014
D0699657
014

FANPIRE

FANPIRE

The Twilight Saga and the Women Who Love It

Tanya Erzen

BEACON PRESS

BOSTON

Beacon Press
25 Beacon Street
Boston, Massachusetts 02108-2892
www.beacon.org

Beacon Press books
are published under the auspices of
the Unitarian Universalist Association of Congregations.

© 2012 by Tanya Erzen
All rights reserved
Printed in the United States of America

15   14   13   12   8   7   6   5   4   3   2   1

This book is printed on acid-free paper that meets the uncoated paper
ANSI/NISO specifications for permanence as revised in 1992.

Text design and composition by Wilsted & Taylor Publishing Services

Erzen, Tanya.
Fanpire : the Twilight saga and the women who love it /
Tanya Erzen.
p. cm.
Includes bibliographical references and index.
ISBN 978-0-8070-0633-7 (hardcover: alk. paper)
1. Meyer, Stephenie, 1973– Twilight saga series. 2. Young
adult fiction, American—History and criticism. 3. Women and
literature—United States—History—21st century.
4. Sex role in literature. I. Title.
PS3613.E979Z644 2012
813'.6—dc23   2012013959

For Matilda and Clive

Author's Note

For the sake of the fans' privacy, I have changed their names and some of their personal characteristics. I use the actual names of public officials in Forks, Washington, and of the creators of fan websites who are well-known figures. There are no composite characters in this book.

Contents

Welcome to the Twilight Zone

As I sit attentively in the lecture "So Many Species, So Little Time: The Men of Twilight," a teenage girl wearily plunks herself down beside me. Rachel's face is obscured by stringy blonde and purple-streaked hair, but I can see her wrists, clad in dozens of black rubber bracelets. One reads, "I'm in love with a fictional character." She scribbles notes, and when she nonchalantly meets my gaze, I see that Rachel's unnaturally golden-brown irises are encircled by orange and black, the result of vampire-inspired contact lenses. Our classroom door has a sign that reads, "No Vampires beyond Here!" and as the talk ends, a scratchy but authoritative voice explodes from the intercom system: "Will Bella Swan please report to the principal's office!" Rachel eagerly confides with me whether she'd like a boyfriend to be a human, vampire, or werewolf. Vampire, or rather the revamped twenty-first-century version of the vampire, wins by a landslide. To Rachel and others like her, he's old-fashioned but still sexy, loyal but tantalizingly dangerous, brooding and anguished about his blood-thirsty nature, young with an artfully disheveled head of hair.

I have officially entered the Twilight Zone, as the banner over the high school where we're sitting proclaims. Rachel is indeed a student, but not here at Forks High School in Washington State, which is hosting a Summer School symposium on the Twilight saga. Rather, she's a self-described "twi-hard," just one of the millions of fervent fans, who range from ages ten to eighty. The beloved series is an ongoing young-adult romance between the exceptionally clumsy teenager Bella Swan and a swoon-inspiring vampire named Edward Cullen, who has been seventeen years old since 1918. Thousands of fans like Rachel have flocked to Forks, Washington, an economically depressed former logging town, eager to immerse themselves in the setting for the books. Forks has responded by remodeling itself as a destination for all things Twilight.

The Twilight "fanpire" spans the globe, but Rachel traveled from Bloomington, Indiana, to be here at the Twilight Summer School. Her obsession with the series began when a friend recommended it to her. Entranced, Rachel spent the night in the bathtub finishing the first book as the water cooled and her skin puckered. She proceeded to tear through the other books in the series, but those weren't enough to satisfy her enthrallment. She logged onto fan sites like *His Golden Eyes* and *Twilighters Anonymous* for at least one hour each day to chat with other fans and peruse the latest Twilight gossip. When I spoke with Rachel at the Summer School symposium, she told me that the current buzz in the fanpire centered around a YouTube video of a recent screening of *Eclipse* where a man proposed to his girlfriend on bended knee in front of the theatre audience. The couple then rejoined the cheering crowd to watch the film.

Rachel's wardrobe consists of Twilight-themed shirts reading, "Bite Me: Vampires Only Please" and "It's an Edward Thing, You Wouldn't Understand." After months of pestering, she'd convinced her mom and her cousins, who'd finally succumbed to Twilight mania, to wait in line at Barnes and Nobles with hundreds of other girls for the midnight release of *Breaking Dawn*, the final book in the series. An enormous poster of Robert Pattinson, the actor who plays Edward, looms over her bed where he watches her sleep. No boy at her high school can pass muster next to the impossibly sparkly perfection of Edward.

Rachel describes the process of reading *Twilight* as being spellbound, a sensation akin to the bliss of encountering a favorite book for the first time. "I don't know what it is about the Twilight series that has captivated me," she tells me. "Once I had read *Twilight*, my life was changed." Fans call this phenomenon *Twitten*, reading the first book and getting bit by the Twilight bug, the inexplicable force that drove them to read all the books in (practically) one sitting. At the elementary school down the block from my house in Washington, fifth graders segregate themselves in the schoolyard according to their allegiances to various male characters, "Team Jacob" or "Team Edward." Friends are forsaken as a result of affiliating with one emblem of eros over another. Other fans dissect the personalities of the Cullens, Edward's fabulously wealthy and attractive vampire family, and bicker over the merits of the Quileute werewolf pack. They write fan fiction, serial novels in countless genres, including the popular "fade to black" fiction with its explicit erotic and sexual details.

Many Twilight fans had never read an entire book before picking up the series, and now they are inhaling it in repeated readings of ten, fifteen, or fifty times. They build websites like *Twilight Singapore*, gay and lesbian fans create Facebook pages dedicated to the series, and through it discover lifelong friends. At conventions, they donate blood, exchange extra Twilight buttons and t-shirts, and bond over bonfires, lunches, and volleyball games. They book tickets for the Twilight cruise to Alaska to mingle with fans and celebrities from the films, read the Twilight graphic novel, meet up with a Twilight mom's group, or buy Twilight merchandise like Sweetarts, a heart-shaped candy that says "bite me" or "soul mate." They wear the au courant raincoat from Nordstrom's Twilight-inspired fashion line. Fans like Rachel do not want to merely read the books; they want to climb inside them and live there.[1]

This book is about the pleasures of the millions of devoted Twilight fans like Rachel who have transformed the Twilight saga into a cultural phenomenon. Thirteen million copies of the books have been sold in the United States; 116 million copies, worldwide, with translations into thirty-seven languages. The film adaptations are some of the highest-grossing movies of all time. Meanwhile, the Twilight saga has spent more time on the *New York Times* best-seller list than even the Harry Potter novels. Its appeal can be encapsulated in the fact that it was recommended to me by my daughter's forty-year-old preschool teacher, a fourteen-year-old neighbor, and a university colleague as must-reads.

Fanpire, one of the collective terms Twilight fans use to describe themselves, evokes the ubiquity and popularity of the Twilight phenomenon, as well as the fact that its readers cross generations, economic strata, and countries. Fans from Romania to Salt Lake City have invented a Twilight-inspired universe that encompasses all aspects of their lives: from Edward-addiction groups and "twi-rock" music to Cullenism, a religion based on the values of Edward's family of vegetarian vampires. There is a lexicon of fan terms: *Twilighter*: a Twilight fan; *Twi-hard*: a die-hard Twilight fan; and *Twibrary*: your collection of all things related to Twilight.

I met fans on tour buses to Twilight-inspired sites; attended thousand-strong conventions; danced at a vampire ball; watched the film premiere of *New Moon* with four thousand primarily Mormon Twilight moms in Utah; befriended people who adorn their bodies with tattoos like the one on the cover of this book; observed vampire baseball games; and struggled through a Bella self-defense class. Approximately 600 people responded to my online fan survey within a few days after some of the major fan websites provided links to it.[2] Their responses, as well as the interviews I conducted with fans in person and online, and my own participation in the fanpire, form the basis of this book.

Is a fan someone who camps out for weeks in a grimy parking lot for a glimpse of a Twilight film star, or is it the person who feels ecstatically transported simply while reading the books? We are all fans of something, whether our fanaticism is private or public, shameful or prideful, steadfast or capricious. Scholars have extensively researched fans and fandoms.[3] Fans are nomadic, and the way they relate to texts is never stable or final. Many travel between fandoms and tastes: young adult fantasy literature, vampire lovers, and romance readers.[4] The fanpire in the United States, based on my online survey, tends to be almost 98 percent women. Eighty percent identify as nondenominational Christians or Catholics while the remainder self-describe as "spiritual." In my survey, 85 percent of respondents were white, and most respondents over age eighteen had completed at least two years of higher education. However, like any amorphous and heterogeneous phenomenon, the fanpire eludes easy classification.[5]

The four books of the series—*Twilight, New Moon, Eclipse,* and *Breaking Dawn*—were written by Stephenie Meyer, a devout member of the Church of Jesus Christ of Latter-Day Saints and a graduate of Brigham Young University who based the narratives on a dream she had of a human girl and a vampire boy lying in a meadow. This paranormal confection of two thousand pages is narrated by Bella, who is sent to live with her father, the police chief of Forks, Washington, after her mother remarries. Bella falls irrevocably in love with Edward Cullen, a mysterious and spectacularly gorgeous student at her high school. He lives with his adopted family of vegetarian vampires who have vowed to feed only on the blood of animals rather than live as monsters who prey on humans. To the townspeople of Forks, the Cullens are merely a rich and attractive doctor's family with five foster children.

Edward is bored and tormented by his ability to read minds. But Bella is the exception, and her mental impenetrability frustrates and captivates him. They meet inauspiciously in biology class as lab partners, where Edward, tempted by the beguiling and unusual scent of her blood, wrestles with his moral values and desire to attack and suck her dry. After a period in which Bella is convinced that Edward despises her, and in which Edward struggles with his warring desires to both protect and devour Bella, he reveals that he is a vampire and that he loves her. "You are exactly my brand of heroin," he says.

Their interspecies romance is plagued by numerous obstacles, like Bella's insecurities (she can never believe someone like Edward could love her) and her predilection for nearly dying on a regular basis, whether at the hands of rival vampires, a motorcycle accident, or a gang of would-be rapists. At the end of the series, Bella and Edward marry and live happily ever after as vampires.

Why do women and girls derive such satisfaction from these particular fantasies of romance and power? Certainly, the Twilight series is a love story between a girl and a vampire, but it also taps into deeper, more pervasive notions about marriage, family, girlhood, sexuality, and celebrity. In Twilight's funhouse mirror, the fears, insecurities, and longings of many girls and women are simultaneously confronted and upended. Your biological family is dysfunctional, abusive, or disconnected, but in Twilight you are embraced by a chosen, nonbiological, and obscenely wealthy family. Your marriage may be disappointing or abusive, but marriage in

Twilight is a supernatural heterosexual model of eternal passion and monogamy. You may be overwhelmed by the American mantra of empowered girlhood that says *you* are responsible for creating your best life, but Bella marries at eighteen, forgoes college, and forsakes her friends because it's her *choice* to do so. You may live with anxieties about whether you can admit to liking or disliking sex without being deemed a slut or a prude, respectively. In Twilight's world, Bella demands and initiates sex without repercussion. Her first time is phenomenal, and it's with someone she is assured will love and respect her forever. You might feel anonymous and insignificant, but Twilight promises that you can become extraordinary. Enchantment lurks around the corner, beckoning in the form of a shimmering, supernatural world where you are desirable and powerful, living vicariously through the character Bella.

The *Goodreads* website produced a map of the United States showing which states have the most Twilight readers. The methodology was flawed because the results were based on self-reporting, but the outcome was telling nonetheless. The map looked eerily like the Red State/Blue State patterns of America's political proclivities that surfaced after the 2000 presidential election. The belt from Texas to North Carolina through the Midwest harbored the highest numbers of positive reviews of the Twilight books. Meanwhile, readers on the coasts rated the series the least favorably. In the states where Goodreads members love the books, abortion is restricted by parental consent and mandatory waiting periods, abstinence-only curricula predominate in high schools, and both teenage pregnancy and adult divorce rates remain higher than the national average.[6]

A series that promotes the alternative world of a boy who insists on preserving his girlfriend's virtue and forces her to wait for sex until marriage because he cares for her soul and safety, and depicts a nonbiological family of married adults who will love and desire each other forever, is the most supernatural aspect of the series. She will remain in the form of a lithe teenage girl without the creeping malaise of middle-age, disillusionment, and financial strain that accompanies marriage over time. The reality is that many girls and women experience failed marriages, a lack of true empowerment, and a cacophony of confusing messages about their sexuality.

What makes Twilight so compelling is its bewildering mix of inverted fantasies and the opposing desires it evokes for fans: Edward is both devastatingly romantic and a creepy stalker. Bella is heroic and a wavering, quavering damsel in distress. The sex or lack thereof harkens back to an era of gentlemanly chivalry, and it can kill you. The Cullen vampires are a model family of *Leave It to Beaver* vampires, yet simultaneously self-obsessed and materialistic. Readers might want to revert to an invented, halcyon past where men waited patiently until after marriage for sex. Or they might identify with an ordinary girl who no longer has to make decisions about her life as she's swept away by the romantic hero. They might also crave some enchantment in their everyday lives. These are the complex desires of the fanpire, and we all live these contradictions in some form daily. They are certainly the fantasies of our contemporary postfeminist moment. Postfeminism, as a form of common sense, tells us that women no longer need economic or political power because women have achieved equality and parity with men, and therefore feminism is redundant and no longer necessary. Scholars have argued that postfeminism is most evident in popular culture, a key site for defining codes of conduct and fostering shifts in social norms.[7] Any choice that women and girls make is indicative of their personal empowerment and freedom, rather than broader constraints like sexism, racism, or economic inequality. The idea that it's daring and commendable for Bella to sacrifice college, friends, family, and even her human life to devote herself to mercurial Edward, all the while asserting that it is her choice to do so, is an exemplar of postfeminist fantasy.

⤐

Are fans merely in love with escapist literature? Because the process of reading can be a rhapsodic form of entertainment does not deprive it of social consequence. The books certainly play a potent role in shaping fans' hopes, ambitions, and expectations, and some of the saga's fantasies are delectable indeed.[8] That such fantasies are appealing to so many girls and women does not mean the fans are bamboozled by the patriarchal messages in the saga, however.[9] Fans are not dupes, nor do they only consume the books uncritically. Their interpretations of the Twilight saga's often-lopsided ideas of gender, sexuality, family, marriage, and celebrity are diverse and evolving. Their paradoxical desires reflect the postfeminist culture in which readers are steeped, where the meanings of empowerment, choice, and fulfillment are constantly evolving.

Romantic fiction has been a popular genre since the publication of Samuel Richardson's *Pamela, or Virtue Rewarded* in Britain in 1740.[10] The demand for modern romance novels in the United States surged in the 1980s, and today, sales of romance novels surpass one billion books annually.[11] The fastest-growing segment of the e-book market is romance, making the plain brown cover my grandmother used to conceal her embarrassment when reading bodice-ripping novels superfluous. The Twilight phenomenon is part of this tradition, but what differentiates it from other romance novel series is the far-flung fanpire the solitary reader can now be a part of. This community is where fans transform the ideas, insignia, and gratification found in their reading into modes of being and sociality that extend into and sustain them in their everyday lives.

The social worlds of Twilight fans are about belonging, enchantment, and contentment with a fantasy that is in many ways deeply antifeminist.[12] For this reason, I look at the effects of pleasure and emotion in fans' experiences of Twilight—and at the disturbing ideas present in the books themselves. I am critical of Twilight, but also viscerally aware of its power to captivate us. The rampantly popular saga commands the devotion of millions of fans, and, as a rare example of popular culture written by and for women, it begs our critical scrutiny.

In the hierarchy of popular cultural topics among most of the people I know, Twilight ranks toward the bottom. Whereas I can discuss *Buffy the Vampire Slayer* or *Battlestar Galactica* with fellow religious studies scholars ad infinitum, and, in fact, have done that very thing, these same colleagues often deride Twilight as insipid or unworthy of our attention. Gradually, the series has inspired numerous scholarly analyses, spoofs, and spin-offs, from SAT-preparation guides to volumes on the philosophical import of Twilight.[13]

We are always implicated in the popular culture we study, whether or not we want to admit it. I sheepishly concede to being utterly beguiled when I watched the first Twilight film in 2008, before I had even read any of the books. Moodily atmospheric and also unintentionally campy, the movie vividly captures the euphoria and angst of high school when having a crush on someone felt all-consuming and earth-shattering. Most of the movie's action occurs in the human world of high school classrooms, field trips, and proms, rather than in the messy world of vampire politics and battles of the later books. *Twilight* has also been the only one of the five film adaptations directed by a woman. Catherine Hardwicke, known for edgier fare like *Thirteen*, brought a tone that was more whimsical and silly than that of later films. But after each subsequent film broke records for highest-opening weekends, Summit Entertainment realized it had an unstoppable franchise on its hands and brought in big-name male directors to helm slicker productions of each subsequent movie adaptation of the books.

Rereading and watching adaptations of Jane Austen's work, in particular *Pride and Prejudice*, is my personal period-piece narcotic. My first viewing of *Twilight* evoked the same guilty thrill I experienced anticipating the inevitable declaration of love after numerous mishaps and misunderstandings in Austen's masterpiece. *Twilight* might lack the witty repartee and droll banter between Elizabeth Bennet and Fitzwilliam Darcy, but unlike the Jane Austen standard wedding scene as love's culmination, the series allows us to witness what happens after marriage—and it isn't the slow dissolution of carnal love amidst child-rearing and aging. In *Twilight*, married people have supernatural sex and maintain passion forever.

After seeing that first film, I attacked the books with gusto, expecting another dose of the same giddy romance. Like many before me, I read them at a breakneck pace—though I drew the line at a marathon bath. I was anxious to know what life-threatening catastrophe might imperil Bella and what improbable twist would wrench her and Edward apart again. Facilitating my reading speed was the books' prose style, sometimes repetitive and riddled with clichés, which doesn't require a reader to linger. Soon, my initial intoxication had been diminished by the overwrought proclamations of undying love and Bella's unrelenting praise of Edward's Adonis-like beauty. Other questions began to intrude persistently as I read: Why can't Bella's father learn to cook and fold his own clothes? Doesn't Bella mind that Edward has been stalking her for months? Or that he's so controlling? Does Edward have to stay away when Bella has her period? Why isn't there a single female character who is unmarried, happy, and intelligent and possesses a sense of humor or a rewarding career?[14]

It brands me as an aberrant fan, but Twilight is the exceptional case in which I prefer the films to the original books, because the most egregious parts of Bella and Edward's already paternalistic relationship are eliminated and the characters have more gumption. Without some of the film's saucy lines, Bella is cloying and boring. And book Edward is immeasurably more patronizing than movie Edward. I missed the tentative guy on screen, who is nervous about showing Bella his bedroom for the first time.

Even if my exhilaration about the film has long since dissipated, it still engenders in me feelings of defensiveness common among Twilight fans, especially since denigrating the fanpire is a favorite pastime for many media outlets. The specter of hundreds of fans shuffling through a mile-long line to obtain an autograph or picture, or clamoring for a glimpse of the film sets, evokes snarky bewilderment among pundits. These women and girls are "hysterical," "rabid," "fanatics," and "obsessed." One publication opined, "*Twilight* fanaticism was as strong as ever this year" while nothing could drown out "the ear-piercing and unexpected sounds of thousands of girls."[15]

At the 2008 Comic-Con, the longstanding convention that is a lure for, mainly, male fans of comics, science fiction, and fantasy, Twilight fans camped out on sidewalks for days to attend the actors' panel. "Fan boy culture's hold on the Con was hijacked by a vampire romance, of all things," said one outraged online commentator.[16] The invasion of female fans into the Comic-Con stronghold even sparked a backlash. A few disgruntled male attendees sported signs that read,

"*Twilight* Ruined Comic-Con." Applying adjectives like "screeching" and "stalking" to fans, commentators implied that Twilight-addicted women should just get a life. It is unsurprising that a phenomenon that massive numbers of women are enthusiastic about is ridiculed as hysteria.[17] But one has to wonder why, for example, equally zealous fantasy-football players or sci-fi geeks, many of whom happen to be male, do not endure the same disdain.

In this book, I explore the various pleasures and disappointments experienced by members of the vast and devoted fanpire in their consumption of all things Twilight. At conventions such as the one discussed in chapter 1, thousands of girls and women discard their cares about boys and men to bond in aerobics and self-defense classes and dance together at elaborate Twilight-themed vampire balls. These women also experience Twilight as a model of choice and empowerment that is actually missing from most of their lives. Married women in the group *TwilightMoms* temporarily abandon domestic responsibilities for convivial sleepovers where they simultaneously bemoan the absence of spicy sex and intimacy in their marriages and reassure themselves that heterosexual marriage is the only way to envision their lives. Chapter 3 follows these women, mainly Mormons, as they ricochet between reckless adolescent feelings and the burdens of domestic responsibility. They didn't mind if Comic-Con was no longer teeming solely with men wearing alien and superhero costumes, nor do they need or want rescuing from the scorn they receive for their fanaticism.

In my time with Twilight fans around the world—from the occasional forum participant and those who watched the films fifty times to the person who corralled her entire office into choosing Team Edward or Team Jacob—I have found they also spoke of how the fanpire transformed their everyday lives, not as mere escapism but as a vehicle for belonging. Twi-bonding is a fan term for the effervescence and connection that families and friends cultivate through the fanpire, and chapter 4 follows a group who travel to Forks, Washington, otherwise known as Twilight's mecca, where enchantment and reality mingle. Impassioned fans wholeheartedly embrace the idea of becoming Cullenists to signify their admiration for the ideal

Cullen family, while some find religious and spiritual succor in the books. Others, hungry for the explicit sex glaringly absent from the Twilight books, pen their own smut stories based on the saga that feature a wanton Bella and lewd Edward engaging in all kinds of lurid sex. Yet, as I note in chapter 4, these stories preserve some of the same assumptions of Twilight, especially the idea that girls should be virginal or sexually inexperienced in order to be worthy of adoration and hot sex, and that the hero, however domineering and hard-hearted he might be, invariably relents and is tamed by his true love and respect for the heroine. Even *Fifty Shades of Grey*, the best-selling romance trilogy about a rich, young CEO in a bondage relationship with a college student, delivers on the romance novel fantasy that a relationship initially based solely on sex will turn into blissful marriage. Before it became a publishing sensation, *Fifty Shades* was "Master of the Universe," the most popular Twilight fan-fiction story online featuring Bella and Edward.

In writing about the fans I met and talked to, I was aware of my tendency to valorize fans' sense of belonging and their resistance to the conservative ideas about gender and sexuality in the books, while minimizing their ravenous consumption of Twilight merchandise.[18] There are Edward and Bella Barbie dolls, calendars, video games, graphic novels, and fangs cleverly promoted and eagerly purchased at conventions and in online stores. As I discuss in chapter 5, the fanpire encompasses authentic ways to belong and connect to others, while it simultaneously and ceaselessly exhorts fans to buy, buy, buy to retain their feelings of enchantment. This reinforces the idea that purchasing power is ultimately the most gratifying expression of fandom. But fans also respond to the franchise through do-it-yourself blogs and homemade crafts that are far from the glossy perfection of Summit Entertainment–approved merchandise. Even these do-it-yourself activities are situated within a commercial context, and there is no clear boundary between where women's desires begin and target marketing ends.

As I write, a replica of Bella's wedding ring, which Edward bestows upon her in *Eclipse*, is one of the most coveted pieces of Twilight merchandise. To entice fans to see *Breaking Dawn–Part 1* again and again, Summit Entertainment promises that by tweeting, "I've seen #BreakingDawn ___ times! #SeeBDAgain," fans might win one for themselves. The fanpire thrives on the fuel of fantasy and delayed gratification. Postponement is the pleasure for fans. The allure is that their desires can never be wholly satisfied, only reproduced over and over through reading, watching and participation in the fanpire.[19] The realization of supernatural true love might never be fulfilled, but they still yearn and hope. That is the liminal state my fellow fan Rachel occupies. Twilight may present a distorted vision of romance and relationships far removed from her daily life, but by embodying and envisioning herself in the Twilight narrative, anything might be possible. She might even receive a marriage proposal in a movie theatre.

I'm in Love with a Fictional Character

Hundreds of girls are rocking out and singing along to "Sexy Vampire," particularly the refrain, which features a classic rock and roll couplet extolling Edward's hotness—"a house on fire"—and rhymes that metaphor with, you guessed it, "sexy vampire." "Squee! I love this song!" someone says. "Squee," to squeal with glee, is the omnipresent sound of an excited fangirl. In this case, they're squeeing about the music of the Bella Cullen Project, a trio comprising Chandler Nash, Ally Kiger, and Tori Randall, high school girls whose acoustic-pop music is inspired by the Twilight books. They're at Twi-Con, the first independent fan convention, held in Dallas, in 2009, and they're about to debut a new song and video called "Safety First," a ballad reveling in the forbidden-yet-fated romance between Bella and Edward.

Chandler, Ally, and Tori are high school juniors who have been playing music together since their days in an Arlington, Texas, church choir. Already a big hit with Twilight fans, the girls have been profiled on MTV and in *People* and *Cosmo Girl*. The Bella Cullen Project credits wizard rock, the music influenced by the Harry Potter phenomenon, for their genesis as a band.

Ally is bookish, with wiry hair, glasses, and a slight build, but she can belt out a song, while Tori is wistful and earnest in black-rimmed glasses on a face that still betrays some of the plumpness of childhood. Chandler Nash, the group's informal leader who has since become a solo artist, has the most "rock and roll" demeanor of the group: her name alone bespeaks a potential run on *American Idol*. She appears world-weary, her bright red lips pursed impatiently, slouched as if she has a guitar slung over her shoulder. With their glasses, scruffy jeans, and t-shirts, and non-gym-toned bodies and freshly scrubbed faces, the Bella Cullen Project members look like slightly nerdy high school students you might catch in the library singing earnest ballads infused with pop. Later this afternoon, people will line up at their TwiCon table to get autographs and snap pictures with them. If the band members seem a bit jaded and tired, it's probably because they've performed at so many Twilight events, and the adulation is nothing new in the world of what they call Vamprock.

Given their moniker, I assume the girls are avid Bella fans, but when I ask, Ally says, "I don't know, we just kind of thought it was a cool name." Ally actually loves the character of Alice, Edward's sister, who has the ability to see the future, a discerning eye for fashion, and a knack for event planning. One of the Bella Cullen Project's new songs is "Pixie with a Gift," an homage to Alice that paints her as a punk-rock princess with a firm grip on her life: she's "the girl with the plan."

In the survey I posted at *BellaandEdward*, a fan site that caters to high school and junior high girls, I'd asked what they thought about the relationship between Bella and Edward, and what qualities they admired about each character. As Chandler, Ally, and Tori did, most girls surveyed chose Alice as the one they would want as a friend. After all, she handpicks designer gowns for Bella and drives a Porsche. Like the Bella Cullen Project song says, she's always got a solution to whatever problem arises. What does she do when Edward is about to commit suicide in Volterra by exposing himself as a vampire to the unwitting residents? She flies there with Bella, steals a car, and rushes Bella to the town plaza to stop him. Alice has moxie. She's courageous and fun. She's punk rock.

Though Alice is the ideal friend, most girls choose Bella as the girl they'd like to be because of her enviable romantic choices. The Bella Cullen Project's song "Switzerland" is based on Bella's attempt to create a truce between the vampires and werewolves, and between her rival suitors, Edward and Jacob. In *Eclipse*, Bella states, "I'm neutral, a peaceful country, Switzerland." The girls sing from Bella's perspective, bemoaning the agony of having to choose between Edward and Jacob. The ongoing Edward-versus-Jacob feud is one of the best-known staples of Twilight fandom: fidelity is indicated by pins and other emblems proclaiming an allegiance to Team Edward or Team Jacob. "Who here is on Team Edward?" followed by whooping, frequently opens workshops and conventions. Alice might have a plan, but Bella, mousy yet beautiful, inexperienced yet able to battle deadly paranormal beings, is the object of desire of a gorgeous vampire and hunky werewolf. Bella gets to choose between Edward and Jacob, and succumb to fated love.

I'd arrived at TwiCon earlier that day on an airport shuttle bus that slowly filled with Twilight fans as we approached the convention center. The girls next to me in the cramped seats, Andie and Jenna, were from Huntsville, Alabama, both in their twenties, and positively gleeful about attending the convention. They kept telling me that this weekend "we get to be kids", and their cell phone ring was the catchy song "Supermassive Black Hole" by Muse, which plays during the first Twilight movie's baseball game scene. Like that of so many others at the convention, their aesthetic could best be described as goth-lite: pink suitcases with skull decals, their hair showing streaks of purple or red, skinny jeans, and t-shirts with Twilight slogans.

Once inside the hotel, the goth-lite effect is magnified a thousandfold. Riding in the elevator, I am crushed between a woman in a gold gown and three-inch heels with a sash designating her as "Queen, Personnel Court," and a heavyset high school girl with fangs and a shirt that reads, "I dream of being with you forever." Momentarily confused, I quickly realize that we are sharing the hotel with a Mary Kay cosmetics convention and their annual awards ceremony overlaps with the first night of TwiCon.

Later, I catch up with Andie and Jenna at the Bella Cullen Project welcome concert in a dimly lit, cavernous room packed with circular tables and a revolving strobe light on the ceiling. After the music winds down, the TwiCon organizers clarify the rules of the convention to the hundreds of girls and women lounging around the room. The main one is to not stalk or take unauthorized pictures of the Twilight actors who will sign autographs the next day.

Andie and Jenna ignore this harangue as Andie enthuses about her clear grasp of Bella's happy situation: "She has two amazing, beautiful men who worship the ground she walks on, who are willing to die for her." Either way, Andie opines, she'll be all right. "It all works out and everything has its proper place, but we don't see that in the beginning, and you have to trust in yourself to make the choices, without that knowledge beforehand, and be true to your heart, because it is all going to work out the way it's supposed to." She goes on to say, "Nothing matters more" than the love between Bella and Edward. Bella's swoony dilemma, I soon discover, is a far cry from the realities of Andie's life. Andie, it turns out, is perpetually stressed out about whether she can afford to go to college outside of her home state or should stay close to home, and whether she'll ever have a boyfriend.

Even if fans acknowledge that Twilight's representation of love is a fictional ideal, the possibility of fated romance triumphing over the messiness and confusion of everyday life are potent. These girls have been told by their teachers, families, and popular culture that they should feel empowered by all the choices available to them. Yet, they also experience anxiety about how to conduct their lives. The allure of Bella is the delicious fantasy of her clear path and of the certainty that love renders her life meaningful and fulfilling. Bella is neither perfect nor glamorous. She's an average teenager like the girls at TwiCon, but her life becomes extraordinary. The girls can hope, imagine, and dream about being a Bella, exchanging the dull conundrums of their lives for an electrifying love affair. The idea of Bella reigns at a time when fans can imagine that they occupy a world in which they have endless options and unlimited freedom. Twilight presents an ideal life, and then exposes Bella as imperfect in its pursuit. What did these girls, dancing to the Bella Cullen Project, awaiting the weekend festivities, take from the books when it came to love and the ideal relationship? What did they envision in their own lives?

Finding Your Inner Bella

The entire TwiCon convention felt like being lost inside a maze of bland plyboard walls and beige carpeting. All the programs and lectures are crammed into one chaotic day, and I have to flip back and forth between multiple pamphlets to figure out whether I should be in the Sheraton Grand Hotel or the convention center across the street. (A few weeks after the convention, the organizers will send a slightly defensive if apologetic letter to the attendees addressing complaints about surly volunteers and the haphazard selection of events.) As I wait in an interminable snaking line to register for the convention, I'm beside Chelsea, a college student making a film about Twilight fans. In front of us is a girl who admits to having spent $10,000 on Twilight merchandise. She zealously clutches the ticket that buys her the chance to meet Kellan Lutz and Jackson Rathbone, the actors who play Edward's brothers, Emmett and Jasper, in the Twilight films.

As we wait, impatiently shifting from foot to foot, a woman spies Chelsea's video camera and begs us to interview her daughter, whom she boasts is a famous web moderator for a Twilight Facebook page. The hitch, apparently, is that the woman's daughter is notoriously shy in person and, at present, hiding in her hotel room. After some cajoling phone calls by her mom, Carly, the young web moderator in question, eventually emerges wearing a button that reads, "Carly Lutz. If found, please return to Kellan."

Carly is initially awkward, shyly biting a nail as she explains how she became the head of one of Facebook's biggest fan groups. But she picks up steam and scarcely draws breath as she veers from how she read *Wuthering Heights* for the first time because of *Twilight* to her goal, inspired by Carlisle Cullen, of becoming a veterinarian. Carly is twenty-one, unemployed, and not planning to go to college (which may impede her career choice). Her major social interactions, outside of participating in her nondenominational Christian church, consist of online friendships with other Twilight fans. "My day is pretty much Twilight all the time," she admits. "I am a really shy person, so people get to know me and, so, doing this whole thing I have gotten to know a lot of people, and I have made a lot of friends. We talk about everything. At first, [the fan forum] just started out at *Twilight*, and we just sort of spawned from there. Now we are all just best friends. It is really fun."

Like the Bella Cullen Project girls and countless others, Carly avers that Bella is just like her. Bella is unpopular and has never had a boyfriend before Edward, and everything about her character subverts the ideal of women who purchase beauty for men's sake. Carly tells me, "Bella is a normal girl that doesn't seem to be overly beautiful or popular. She actually seems to be quite the opposite, clumsy and self-conscious." Andie put it this way: "I am such a Bella. Like, I know it's way overused and everyone thinks they're a Bella, but really, the clumsiness, the book-worminess, I'm such a Bella. I mean, Jenna?" Jenna confirms it: "You are. She's a klutz. She's always in her head, I swear, not paying attention and stutters a lot, doesn't know what to say most of the time, panics easily." Thousands of girls are Bellas. The feat of the books is that Meyer has created in Bella a character so unremarkable, yet so desirable, that anyone can project herself onto her.

The insecurity of someone like Carly, who feels most comfortable interacting with others virtually, is mirrored in Bella's chronic self-doubt, which continues unabated throughout the series until, in the final book, she becomes a vampire. Bella continually questions how Edward could possibly love her and disparages her own abilities. Self-effacing and lacking confidence, Bella tells Edward in *New Moon*, "I don't trust myself to be . . . enough. To deserve you." Jenna and Andie admire Bella because she is self-deprecating, honest, humble, and average, not exactly the characteristics of a typical Hollywood heroine. Tired of constant exhortations to bolster their own self-image with weight loss, makeup, and hollow charm, these young women realize, with Bella, that being overweight or nerdy or having bad skin isn't necessarily a detriment if you can still find the only guy for you in the universe. Young Twilight fans, enduring the agonies of high school, identify with the bumbling teenage girl with divorced parents stuck in the boondocks. Carly says, "She is just a normal girl. Someone I can relate to. . . . She has found her soul mate and very simply . . . wants to live with him, stay with him for the rest of eternity."

Bella is the antithesis of the way so much of popular culture expects women to look. She is plain and oblivious to fashion yet the object of devoted romance and love. She provides a vivid template upon which girls like Carly, Andie, and Jenna displace their own disillusionment with the expectations of sexualized, consumption-driven girlhood. Girls at the TwiCon said of Bella: "She doesn't care what she's wearing or how her hair looks." And, "She's not a glamazon; she's real." And, "I like that she isn't your typical stupid, self-centered, vain teenage girl." Bella isn't the alpha girl, just the ordinary girl. Carly concurs: "She is a normal teenager and has the same insecurities that a lot of girls have, and she isn't some little bimbo who is stunning and perfect." Bella is that girl sweating and awkwardly flailing around during gym class. "I'm absolutely ordinary—well, except for bad things like all the near-death experiences and being so clumsy that I'm almost disabled," Bella says in *Twilight*.

There are about sixty versions of this girl on the thirty-seventh floor where I'm heading to "Cardio with the Cullens," or, aerobics a la Twilight. To get there, I brave the dreaded elevators, waiting a half hour for one that can actually accommodate another person. Thus begins another excruciatingly cramped journey squeezed between Twilight fans and Mary Kay saleswomen. Once in the room, the expansive views of downtown from the floor-to-ceiling windows feels liberating, and even nondescript Dallas glimmers invitingly. The windows and wall of mirrors transform the space into a giant dance studio and almost make me believe the program blurb that exercising while mimicking Twilight characters "will make your blood sing."

The girls and women, who appear to range in age from about twelve to forty-five, wear mismatched combinations of jeans, tights, and t-shirts (with slogans like Team Edward: Some Like It Chilly and Cullen-Lovin' Nut), kick, gesticulate, complain, and laugh. Leading the class in complicated combinations of aerobics moves and urging them to "Jaspercize" are Kiera and Liz, known by fans of their Twilight parody website as the TwiCurls due to their unruly hair. The popular sister-act are dressed ironically in aerobics clothes circa 1987: long t-shirts knotted on the side and spandex black tights.

Kiera is pregnant, but that doesn't deter her from running the class like a perky drill sergeant. Each part of the routine is based on the actions of a member of the Cullen family as they play baseball in the pivotal scene from *Twilight* when nonvegetarian vampires threaten Bella. We all recite: "Carlisle, Carlisle [arm up], Alice [kick and pitch], Jaasssssper [circle your arm around, run like Edward and turn around [run in place and jump to face the opposite direction], monkey-man, monkey-man [hopping back and forth on each foot]" to imitate Emmett, Edward's other brother.

I begin to flounder when Liz, bouncing sprightly on her toes, adds the "Newton shuffle" by shimmying up and down like Bella's classmate Mike Newton did outside the diner while Bella and her dad are eating, in a scene from the first Twilight film. Kiera yells, "You don't care if Bella's dad is watching." We throw ourselves into the clever routine with abandon while complaining good-naturedly, relishing how each move is an inside joke for those intimately familiar with the series.

"Cardio with the Cullens" enables these girls to revel in and embody Bella's qualities. In the Twilight saga, Bella flails and is often clownishly uncoordinated, to the extent that she trips over her own feet. In many of the workshops at TwiCon, such as "Alice's Makeover Room" and "Twilight Party Decorating," the hope is that somewhere out there (though certainly not at TwiCon, where I've spotted fewer than ten males) a man-boy like Edward awaits. He might choose you in the way he chose Bella. After all, as Chandler, Tori, and Ally sing, Bella is, according to Edward, the "most beautiful girl you'll ever see/She's the best part of me." While the idea of the workshop is that women and girls, even the twelve year olds, should be fit and pretty, it also emphasizes a klutzy, inept version of aerobics where you perspire and look silly without anyone caring. The workshop is a release valve for glee and abandon, a space for fun and goofiness, where being clumsy is actually cool. I'm struck by how the self-consciousness that afflicts girls evaporates, especially since we're in a room where you can't avoid watching yourself in the unforgiving mirrors.

"Bella is ready for all of us to slow it down, take it to the meadow for a cool-down," Kiera tells us. "Focus on your core, because if you're Bella, you're going to lose it when you go into *New Moon*," poking fun at Bella's nervous breakdown when Edward leaves her in the second Twilight book. Breathless, Kiera has us repeat Edward's famous line to Bella: "You're like a drug to me." Then each of us turns to another girl in the room for affirmations. "You've completed the workout, you deserve praise and affirmation. Turn to the partner and say, 'You are my life now,'" another classic Edward line. Each girl holds hands with another until everyone in the room is linked in a winding chain.

Afterward, most of the women and girls wait to have their pictures taken with the TwiCurls. Kiera and Liz comically enact various poses from the books, but the one that garners the most laughs is another dig at Edward, what Liz calls the "stalker pose" in which they crouch over two young girls with their hands in the air as if they're going to attack. "I mean, Edward Cullen is not a perfect man," Kiera tells me. "He is a creeper! He's stalking [Bella]. He's almost, like, overly territorial sometimes. I mean, he can be way too sullen and moody." After the photo session, the crowd disperses, and the next slew of animated girls and women enters for another session.

Surefire Lives

As I leave the aerobics class, I notice four girls sprawled in the corner of the hotel lobby. They've given up on getting anywhere because of the elevator madness and are eating an impromptu lunch on the floor after the cardio session. Hannah and Gabriella, nineteen-year-olds from Austin, Texas, have just met Diane, a thirty-year old mom from Mississippi, and Lara, an eighteen-year-old from Woodstock, New York. I join them and find that they're bonding over the delirious fact that they all love Twilight and how distinct their fandom is from others. Hannah, the most outspoken of the bunch, says, "I'm not a Trekkie. I am normal." Those who disparage the fanpire, she says, are "just jealous because we have something cooler to be a fan of." The young women intermittently and proudly refer to themselves as "Twilight freaks," relishing having all met just ten minutes ago.

Diane, who has left her small child with her in-laws to be here, says it's rejuvenating for her to spend time with others who share her passion. "Like, all of a sudden you're not, like, the only one who is obsessed."

Hannah jumps in: "Yeah, you're not considered a freak because you read the book."

The young women can good-naturedly argue over whether they prefer Team Edward or Team Jacob, but "still, it's friendly," says Lara. "It's not like you're going to get into a fistfight." Initially, Lara was reluctant to read the books since "preppy girls" liked them, she says, but once she did, she realized they were about her and her friends. At TwiCon, Lara and the girls can let their freak flags fly, meeting others with the same vampire infatuation, preppy or not, sharing lunches with them in the halls, and exchanging arcane Twilight trivia, and no one blinks an eye.

Our conversation takes on a range of topics; the girls finish each other's sentences, jumping in to make a point, or they just ramble. We talk about whether the Twilight books make a difference in their non-Twilight lives. Like so many other fans, they all attest to their inner Bellas. "She's not perfect. She's like, pretty much, like every teenage girl," says Lara with a sigh. Hannah adds, "She's the prettiest with extraordinary traits." Hannah desists from joking only when the conversation shifts to sex, or the lack thereof in the book series. She complains that, in the real world, sexual standards keep changing, and it is impossible to know what young women are supposed to do. "You should be sexual," she says, "but then you're told not to have sex. It's just very confusing."

"Yeah," Gabriella agrees, "you need to be slutty, you need to be trampy, you need to wear this tiny piece of clothing and get [boys] all turned on, but then tell them no. But when you tell them no, [it's], Here's a condom, to make sure you are safe. What are you saying?"

At least for these four young women, reading the Twilight series provides a reprieve and an escape from all these choices. Diane, the thirty-year-old mom, explains, "You read a book, you get lost in it. You go someplace else. Like, to forget what your worries [are], forget this stuff." The conundrum of what kind of girl or woman they are supposed to be is echoed by others at TwiCon and in the hundreds of responses to my survey.

On her official website, Twilight series author Stephenie Meyer writes that true feminism is about choice. It means, she says, that a woman can do whatever will bring her the most happiness. The pressure on girls like Hannah to make the right choices and build a successful life is intense. The idea of "girl power," whether it comes from the corporate boardroom or the National Organization for Women, is that young women can be anything they want, and that there are now countless options available to them. But as Hannah points out, those options are often confusing and contradictory. The proponents of girl power present the idea that girls are assertive, dynamic, and unencumbered by the constraints of femininity. At the same time, popular books like Mary Pipher's *Reviving Ophelia* warn that girls are vulnerable, voiceless, and fragile. Both concepts place the onus for girls' lives solely on their individual choices and personality traits rather than on structural explanations for girls' inequality and the double standards that plague them.[1] Girl power is proffered as the gentle and nonthreatening alternative to feminism, so that girls view the contradictions in their lives as a result of their own personal failures rather than as part of social and political realities.

Popular culture in particular tells girls that they are empowered precisely because they now possess freedom and innumerable choices, and if they fail in our age of immeasurable possibility, it's simply their fault.[2] "Individuals must now choose the kind of life they want to live. Girls must have a lifeplan," argues girlhood scholar Angela McRobbie. "They must become more reflexive in regard to every aspect of their lives, from making the right choice in marriage, to taking responsibility for their own working lives."[3] The staggering array of so-called choices leaves many girls feeling rudderless and confused, like Hannah, trying to figure out how to dress and when to have sex.

McRobbie contends that the state, the media, and popular culture converge in the production of a wide range of messages that convey the idea that individual girls bear the sole responsibility for the course of their lives. It is an "ethos of self-perfectibility through endless personal effort and self-monitoring,"[4] rather than any attempt to think about the broader constraints upon the lives of girls. Andie may want to go to college, but she can't afford it, and her family's demands prevent her from relocating too far away anyway. This logic of empowerment through choice is now seen as a matter of common sense, treated as self-evident by a generation of girls. But the logic is also double-edged.

Further, the idea of choice is for many an illusion of postfeminism. In actuality, as girlhood studies scholars have demonstrated, most girls don't have an abundance of choices at all, and the idea that it's up to the individual to make her way masks real inequalities in regard to race, class, gender, and sexuality. These mythical choices of careers, college, and the right relationships are only available to girls with certain privileges.[5]

Hannah, Diane, and others long for lives with guarantees, not ones that feel unsettled and precarious. I was struck by how many girls I encountered, both at Twilight events and in my survey, who admitted to being weary of making decisions. Exhausted by being in charge, they expressed a craving to have someone else—specifically, a boy—do it. "I'm always the one that dominates a relationship. And I'm tired of it," Lara said to me. Of Edward, Hannah says, "I couldn't dominate him. He's an older and smarter person, and is a lot stronger. Plus, I think I would do anything he asked of me."

Diane complains about the stress of having a young child: "I am more of the provider, and the idea of being taken care of is more appealing." The fantasy of having the life of a heroine like Bella, who relinquishes her autonomy and feels pleasure against her will in the process, a staple of older forms of romance fiction, may be deeply appealing to these young women. It gives readers permission to abdicate control vicariously and provides a reprieve from the control they are forced to exercise in their lives.

For them, reading is an escape into a world where life is fated for happiness. Bella is the lucky girl, one who appears to have many enviable options—whether to become a vampire, whether to be with Jacob or rush off to Italy to save Edward. She decides to prioritize true love, assured that this is her destiny. Bella's life boils down to the question of how she can be with Edward forever. Although she is presented with choices, it is always clear that, in her case, true love trumps everything else. The best relationships, according to the mores of the Twilight series, are the ones in which girls don't have to make decisions because love is so easy and receiving affection is so imbued by fate.

One of many similar exchanges in *Twilight* between Edward and Bella goes like this:

> [EDWARD:] "As long as it makes you happy, I'll be here." . . .
> [BELLA:] "You're talking about forever, you know."

Bella isn't so much empowered by her choices as compelled to make them. Her love *for* Edward is the source of her self-assurance, even if she lacks confidence *in* him and others. "Once she makes her decision, she sticks to it . . . there's no turning back," said one girl I spoke with at the TwiCon. The question is how much of her decision is really hers and how much is the result of Bella being caught up in Edward's will.

Damsels, Glamazons, and Black-Belt Bellas

In *New Moon,* the second book in the saga, Edward abandons Bella rather than risk consuming her in a vampiric frenzy, and she lapses into a catatonic state of grief for months. She tempts death by motorcycle riding and cliff diving just to conjure up Edward's voice in her head, a voice that chastises her for endangering herself in the name of love. But if Bella can't be with Edward, she'd rather risk life and limb to at least be able to hear him berate her. In reference to this part of the book, Jenna told me that Bella "is a great role model, in my opinion, for her independence, survival, and ability to not hold grudges." Jenna praised Bella's selflessness, stubbornness, and initiative in her relentless campaign to convince Edward to make her immortal. Bella's status as a role model apparently rests on her willingness to sacrifice herself for her family, Edward, and others. In response to my online survey, some said about Bella: "She always puts everyone first before herself," and, "She's the 'suffer in silence' type. She chooses her own pain over others'."

Young women like Hannah the TwiCon attendee understand Bella as an unlikely and scrappy heroine who often saves herself and others despite her ineptitude. "She is clumsy and seems like the damsel in distress," Hannah says, "but she can hold herself [together] and be the hero if needed." She stops Edward from committing suicide and protects him from the evil vampire aristocracy, the Volturi, with her impermeable mind.

Lara disagrees, calling Bella "a weak Mary-Sue character that gets too much attention from too many males," and accuses the character of being "clingy and needy." Jenna tells me that Bella "should have been given more ambition. She never does go to the bookstore; she never does go to college."

As readers, we are told repeatedly that Bella is smart and strong, but her actions, or rather the actions that happen *to* her, only illustrate her frailty. Bella stumbles constantly, faints in school, and is victimized three times in the first book alone, all the while blaming herself for her troubles.

To the girls in the fanpire, Bella's worst crime is her metamorphosis from klutz to glitzy and gorgeous vampire, and her abandonment of average girls like them. "I did not like the way she changed. I can understand; she became a vampire, so she was superconfident, but it was such an extreme. She lost Bella somewhere in there," Hannah says.

Gabriella agrees. "I liked the shy, kind of scared, kind of nervous, clumsy [person]," she says, "and I can understand the whole 'She's not clumsy anymore' [transformation]. But there wasn't Bella after she changed into a vampire. That's the Bella we fell in love with."

In general, though the young women at TwiCon admired the possibility of becoming powerful, exquisite, and beloved by a dream man, most realized that what happened to the girl in the books would never happen for them, and that felt like a betrayal. Despite the abundance of merchandise, I never saw anyone at TwiCon wearing a t-shirt or pin with "Team Bella" on it, even though Kristen Stewart, the actress who plays her in the Twilight movies, has a fan base that includes "Krisbians" (Kristen + Lesbian = Krisbian). There is also a blog devoted to girls who are "gay for Kristen" even if they don't all identify as lesbians, just as there are sites such as GayforTay for men who lust after Taylor Lautner, the actor who plays Jacob Black.

Heroine or victim? The contradiction was exemplified by the subject of my next workshop, Bella's Self-Defense Class. Even after my interlude with Hannah, Lara, and Diane, the elevators are still disgorging passengers at an alarming rate. In exasperation, I tramp down thirty-one flights of stairs, accompanied by two girls and their mother. Chatting about the convention makes the descent bearable, and I end up in the lobby where I gratefully collapse onto a bench. Unfortunately, the self-defense class will require my physical participation, but at least I can avoid another elevator ride to get to it since it's on the ground floor.

When I arrive, a bit late after waiting for my leg tremors to subside, I find myself in another huge conference room with floor-to-ceiling windows and every space occupied by girls reclining on the floor. Taught by Marissa, a member of *TwilightMoms* and a black belt in tae kwon do and hapkido, the session commences with a PowerPoint presentation garnished with quotes from the Twilight books about the way Bella defends herself.

The conceit for our class comes from a scene in *Twilight* when Bella finds herself alone in Port Angeles after dark and narrowly escapes being assaulted by a group of rapists. As Bella tries to flee, she realizes, "I wasn't being followed. . . . I was being herded." Marissa reminds us of how Bella prepares to scream, but her throat is dry and her voice is shaky. The fifty girls and women in class are familiar with Bella's internal monologue in *Twilight*: "I brace myself, feet apart, trying to remember through my panic what little self-defense I knew." As the men encircle her, she recalls her training and prepares to use her hand to break one's nose, put a finger through the eye socket of another, and knee the groin of yet another. "I wasn't going out without taking someone with me," Bella says. "I tried to swallow so I could build up a decent scream."

But fate intervenes again, and none of Bella's self-defense training needs to be put into action because Edward careens around the corner, flashing his headlights and ordering her into his silver car while he growls at the would-be attackers, sending them off. He is the Knight in the Shining Volvo.

Marissa, who is sturdy and strong with her long, black hair in a braid, explains that what Bella did well in that situation was to stay calm and trust her instincts. However, she warns us to avoid walking alone in unfamiliar streets at night, being unaware of our surroundings, and having no means of escape. Since most of us can't rely on a vampire swain for assistance, it's time to learn to fight for ourselves. First, Marissa teaches us her SAM technique: Sight, Airway, Mobility. "Interrupt the vision, interrupt the breathing, and interrupt the balance by attacking the weakest points like the eyes, nose, mouth, throat, and groin," she says. Marissa admonishes the more enthusiastic participants, including one girl who is practicing roundhouse kicks: "You aren't trying to be Jackie Chan. You just want to get away as soon as you can." The girls are engrossed, listening to her advice to always travel in groups, walk confidently, and make eye contact because would-be attackers prey on timid women.

In a no-nonsense but patient manner, Marissa parries their questions: "Can you bite him?" *"Yes, bite his bicep off."* "What if he has a gun or is much bigger?" *"Don't wrestle the attacker, because you will lose."* "What if they have a chokehold on you?" *"Drive your chin down."* "What is the best place to hit or grab?" *"The groin, the groin, the groin, the groin."* The girls recite "groin" like a mantra.

Arrayed in a lopsided circle, we strike outward with the heel of our hands while yelling, "Heeeyah!" Although she was demure in our lunch conversation, here Diane intently follows the instructor's every move as if her life depended on it. There is no choreographed routine or right way to do this. Marissa points out: "It's not aerobics. You just want to get away. If you're busy worrying about the right move, you are going to get hurt." Unlike the laughter in the cardio class, here everyone is focused and intent, grunting with each arm thrust.

Marissa wants us to envision ourselves as a black-belt Bella, who, drawing on her SAM training, repels attackers of both the human and supernatural variety. At the same time, Bella is almost always portrayed as vulnerable and continually in need of saving, whether from evil, homicidal vampires like James (*Twilight*); near-drowning and motorcycle mishaps (*New Moon*); James's vengeful lover, Victoria, and her newborn army (*Eclipse*); or from her own clumsiness (every book). Even if in *Twilight* Bella says, "I can't always be Lois Lane. I want to be Superman, too," she is perpetually in need of protection from Edward or Jacob.

Marissa also neglects to mention that Edward is only able to extract Bella from her assailants in the first place because he's been stalking her for months. The sexual assault information Marissa includes at the end of her presentation is important, but it overlooks a central problem with the series: Edward is a controlling, manipulative, and downright creepy boyfriend at times. And most violence against women is perpetrated by people they know. Why not tell us what to do if a boyfriend slips into your window without your knowing? Or if someone forces a kiss on you, as Jacob does to Bella? Yet, in *Twilight*, when Edward comes to her aid in Port Angeles, Bella says she feels safe, even though it's obvious that Edward was only able to rescue her because he'd been following her. "It was amazing how instantaneously the choking fear vanished," she says, "amazing how suddenly the feeling of security washed over me—even before I was off the street—as soon as I heard his voice."

Stalker Edward

In his trademark domineering and protective way, Edward forbids Bella to enter the woods without him, chastises her for her inclination to get into trouble, and slips into her room to watch her sleep before they are a couple. One girl wrote the following in response to my online survey about Twilight: "Edward is a bit over the top and at times it's creepy because real women think that if a man follows you around and watches you sleep that's okay. . . . It's not and they really need to get out of the relationship." Edward's behavior is supposed to be acceptable because he ultimately has Bella's best interests in mind, but as a girl in the self-defense class says, "Edward is ridiculously controlling." In the books, Edward's belittling lines directed at

Bella are rampant, such as these two from *Eclipse*: "You aren't exactly the best judge of what is or isn't dangerous," and, "Please make a conscious effort to keep yourself safe. I'll do everything I can, but I would appreciate a little help."

Nevertheless, most of the fanpire girls and women view Edward's control issues as part of his old-fashioned charm. His charisma, icy marble muscles, and undeniable gorgeousness enable them to overlook his paternalism, though it is his paternalism that makes him so appealing to fans. He inspires torrents of gushing adjectives in female fans, while they simultaneously half-heartedly criticize him for being a "stalker, creep, or control freak." A fan wrote to author Jana Riess, author of the *Flunking Sainthood* blog on Beliefnet, admonishing her for criticizing the gender roles in the series: "What's wrong with looking for a knight in shining armor?" Riess responded with a series of rhetorical questions: Would you want your knight to stalk your movements daily, slam you against a wall at full force, break up with you with no explanation and leave you in the woods to die of hypothermia, pin your wrists down and keep a hand over your mouth so you can't speak, hire someone to kidnap you so you can't visit a romantic rival, bruise your entire body after the first time you have sex?[6]

For many girls, the resounding answer was "Absolutely, yes."

Midway through the self-defense class, four women in their early thirties strut in, huddle together, and watch the proceedings. With their gold jewelry, trendy balloon pants, tank tops, and faux Louis Vuitton bags, they are the flash to the frump of most of us at Twi-Con. Polly from Wichita Falls, Texas, has a master's degree in teaching, though her friend Christie never finished reading a book until *Twilight* and has now read the series twenty times by her accounting. Polly and Christie appear uninterested in the class, sitting together on a bench on the side.

Polly, Christie, and Jan, another of the late arrivals, abandon their nonchalance when I later ask them about Edward, however. "He's handsome, devoted, and nothing else matters [to him] except Bella," Christie says, while Polly refers almost affectionately to him as a psycho and stalker. The very fact that Edward is "perfect and not so perfect at the same time" is also what makes him beguiling, Christie says. Polly adds that she's never been attracted to the "bad boy with a conscience," except with Dylan, the iconic loner from the 1990s popular television series *Beverly Hills, 90210.* According to Christie, it's sexy that Edward watches Bella without her knowing. Jan enumerates his best traits: "He is selfless, patient, kind, loving, beautiful, strong, honest, and humble," while Christie adds, "Charm, intelligence, gentlemanliness, humor, selflessness, chivalry, love for his family." Someone answering the survey wrote that Edward is "hot, he can play the piano, he can read minds, he is so selfless, he does whatever he can to make Bella happy. HE DRIVES AN ASTON MARTIN VANQUISH!!!!" The character of Edward and, to a certain extent, that of Robert Pattinson, the actor who plays him in the Twilight movies, is universally admired and lusted after in the fanpire.

The possessor of superhuman strength, a spectacular appearance, the ability to read minds, and tousled hair, Edward sweeps Bella off her feet and protects her from life's uncertainties. He's amassed wealth over time, so Bella will never have to worry about financial security or a job. He possesses the wisdom of a century trussed up in a teenager's body. And he sparkles. Fans use "OME," for "Oh my Edward!" a term comparable to "Oh my God!" They're "Robsessed," "addicted to Edward," and "in love with a fictional character," all of which are also the names of various Twilight blogs and websites. Despite Stephenie Meyers's contention never to have read vampire books or romance fiction, Edward bears a strong resemblance to the recent heroes of paranormal romance: supernaturally strong and emotionally vulnerable.[7] The latter characteristic is evinced in his maudlin lines from *New Moon*: "If I could dream at all, it would be about you. And I'm not ashamed of it."

In this and other ways, the Twilight series slyly subverts some stereotypical notions of masculinity. Throughout the books and films, and in the copious merchandise, for instance, it is male bodies that are thrillingly objectified the way women's typically are in Hollywood fare. Fans ogle Edward and Jacob, who are frequently shown or described as shirtless, while Bella remains clad in jeans except for an occasional tasteful dress. We read ceaseless descriptions of Edward's "marble" beauty and Jacob's enhanced muscles after he becomes a wolf-pack member. Page after endless page, Bella rhapsodizes that Edward is "dazzling" and "flawless" with "hypnotic eyes" and a "magnetic" personality. In *Twilight*, she says, "I wasn't interesting. And he was. Interesting . . . and brilliant . . . and mysterious . . . and perfect . . . and beautiful . . . and possibly able to lift full-sized vans with one hand." One anti-Twilight saga blog even tallied up the amount of time Bella spends obsessing about Edward's physical attributes; references to his eyes, chest, skin, face, voice, and hair numbered in the hundreds.

> "You're doing it again," [Bella] muttered. . . .
> "What?"
> "Dazzling me," I admitted. . . .
> [Edward] frowned. "Oh."
> "It's not your fault," I sighed. "You can't help it."
>
> —from *Twilight*

Vampire Romeo

In the survey on *BellaandEdward*, I asked readers which relationship in the Twilight books they would most like to emulate and why. Almost 85 percent of the more than 1,500 respondents said it was Bella and Edward's. (The rest preferred Jasper and Alice's.)

In their song "Safety First," the Bella Cullen Project girls sing from Bella's perspective about why she loves "the monster" and how she shouldn't want him and he shouldn't want her. Then the song's perspective shifts from Bella's to Edward's, proclaiming that nothing else matters more than their love and that she's the best part of him. It's the ultimate romantic power ballad for every teenage girl.

"She gives me hope that I, too, will one day have a relationship like she and Edward have," Jenna tells me. When I was chatting with Hannah, Lara, Gabriella, and Diane at TwiCon, they discussed how they started reading Shakespeare because of Twilight, and Hannah said she finally got around to reading *Pride and Prejudice* after reading *Twilight* for the third time. "And I loved it," she says. "And I loved *Wuthering Heights*. . . . I like the way [Heathcliff and Cathy] never really give up on each other. And it's too easy in the real world to give up on people." Lara chimes in: "I'm a hopeless romantic myself." Adds Hannah, "Yeah, everyone just gets this bubbly feeling and sort of, like, 'I want that.' It's a hopeful kind of thing."

They agreed that "love conquers all" and repeatedly remarked that Bella and Edward had overcome obstacles to be together, the primary one being his vampire nature and her humanity. They talked of the relationship's "intensity" and how it was "meant to be" even if forbidden. "The relationship between Edward and Bella is the relationship I dream of having myself," says Jenna. "Although it seems almost impossible, that very fact makes it desirable." According to Jenna, Edward and Bella's relationship is the only one in the Twilight books "that actually has true love in it."

Scholars have noted that cultural representations of romance shape teenage girls' perceptions of ideal relationships and potential partners.[8] What makes Twilight captivating for these young women is that Bella and Edward's relationship endures suffering and sacrifice, thus granting it authenticity. In this, it isn't just a fantasy to them but something akin to an actual relationship. Ally of the Bella Cullen Project band tells me at TwiCon, "I think that you've got to see the whole picture of it because, you know, Bella and Edward have the wonderful, like, they're-in-love relationship, but they have problems too, like every relationship does. Like, you know, true love does happen. What I like about the books is that it shows that relationships do not always have a picture-perfect bow. They do have trials and tribulations."

The ideal relationship that *Twilight* presents for girls and young women is all-consuming and invariably necessitates suffering. As Edward tells Bella in *New Moon*, "The odds are always stacked against us. Mistake after mistake. I'll never criticize Romeo again." Jenna says, "They both love each other so much that they would endure horrific amounts of pain just so the other didn't have to." The young women continually use words like "sacrifice" and "work" as the ultimate expression of romance. As one of my Internet respondents declared, "There is passion, protection, and heartbreak in

[Bella and Edward's relationship], everything a girl looks for." Making true love last requires a herculean effort, and relationships involve misunderstandings and insurmountable difficulties, another trope of romance novels.[9] One young woman said that Bella and Edward "have the kind of love that is meant to be, because it takes work. The love that came easily for the rest doesn't have the appreciation of a love that you have to work for. My husband was in Iraq so I know how it feels to have to fight yet be patient for love."

Jenna and Andie, like many I spoke with at the TwiCon, said they thought Bella would have had a healthier relationship with the character Jacob, a human for whom she does not have to become a vampire or abandon her family, friends, or plans for college. Ally of the Bella Cullen Project told me, "I think Bella's a better person when she's with Jacob. . . . She just doesn't seem so needy. She opens up and really becomes herself when she's with Jacob and she kind of closes up and becomes something that she thinks Edward wants." Bella is free-spirited and reckless with Jacob. Their relationship revolves around friendship because they actually know and respect one another before Jacob declares his love for her.

On the other side, Team Edward fans are partially seduced by a Romeo and Juliet vision of romance: instead of the messy and complicated choices of girlhood, they can imagine being swept away by the romantic hero. A powerful and sensitive man will materialize to carry them off their feet and protect them from life's vicissitudes. As the multimillion-dollar market in romance novels attests, this vision of escapist romantic fantasy isn't limited to Twilight. However, in terms of Bella's sense of empowerment, it is hard not to judge the vision of relationships in the Twilight saga as a paltry one.

Instead of going to college, Bella becomes a wife and mother, albeit supernatural ones, at age eighteen. Her independence evaporates in the face of her vampire romance. Despite her alleged intelligence and love of reading, her life is devoid of any interest other than Edward, and the hours spent away from him are torture to her. Bella experiences trepidation about marriage at such a young age but succumbs because Edward insists that marriage is the price they must pay to have physical intimacy.

Twilight Guys

At TwiCon, I set out with Chelsea, the student making a film about fans, to interview Kaleb Nation, the self-proclaimed Twilight Guy, who has become a minor sensation within the fanpire. An enterprising and slightly nerdy twenty-two-year-old from Texas, Nation has found a niche posting irreverent interpretations of each successive chapter from "the guy perspective." His blog has over 4 million registered users, and he is now the author of his own young adult fantasy series. When I catch up with him, he materializes from behind a pillar in the lobby. As we step on the elevator, he glances around furtively. Someone, he confides, is stalking him. I'm skeptical, but then a girl appears on the mezzanine level and stares at him fixedly. Kaleb tells us to rush past her, and I realize the girl is Hannah, whom I ate lunch with after the cardio session.

We arrive unscathed by further interruptions in a quiet room on the now-deserted thirty-seventh floor (most everyone else is in the convention hall waiting to get autographs from the films' actors). Kaleb, his brown hair flopping in his face, reminisces with self-deprecation about how he facetiously wrote a blog post that Summit Entertainment should cast him to play Edward in the first Twilight film. A flood of outraged e-mail ensued. He refers affectionately to crazy fans but also admits his own guilt and embarrassment about being male in an almost entirely female fandom.

"I knew I had to read these books," he says. "I had to find out what was in this series that bewitched so many of these girls into this obsession." In order to obtain a copy of Twilight, Kaleb ordered it online so no one would see him holding it in a bookstore; he rejected picking it up at the library for the same reason. "It came to my house in a discreet cardboard box, which I opened in my bedroom behind locked doors," he says. "In fact, even after I finally had it inside [my room], I kept the cover turned around in my bookshelf so that the spine was not visible to my friends." Kaleb believes that it is something greater than Edward's sparkly skin or muscles that captivates fans and makes the Twilight saga more than a fad. "Would he be loved so much if he was still so attractive and yet selfish and uncaring to Bella?" Kaleb says. The reason, he authoritatively announces, is "true love. Love can break down any barriers. It says true love defies all odds, natural and supernatural, that it exists somewhere."

As the confidant and source of advice for male fans who are too ashamed to admit they read the books, Kaleb says they frequently ask him how to become more like Edward. He doesn't have a good answer. "How [can] I be like Robert Pattinson and never brush my hair or shower and still have millions of girls that want me? I still have not figured that out," he says. "One of the best things about running a site for Twilight was that it connected me with guys all over the world who have read the books and many others who were struggling to understand their Twilighter girlfriends. Sometimes I would get frantic e-mails from guys begging me for advice on how to get their girlfriends back from this fictional character named Edward Cullen."

Kaleb's role as a dispenser of advice for men solidifies his place as the male expert on Twilight without impugning his masculinity or heterosexuality. He and other male fans want to know about the series to understand potential girlfriends, but many are secret fans as well, and seeking advice about girls is a guise for their own love of Twilight. The fandom is so female-dominated that *Twilight Guy* is the only forum where they can comfortably ask advice and share their thoughts.

But what happens when girls in love with Edward's idea of romantic courtship interact with the average high school guy? In high school, most of the boys are decidedly unlike Edward. Jenna's boyfriend always acted "distant," she says, and she longed to have with him the emotional intimacy she shared with her friends. To her dismay, she once caught her boyfriend looking at online porn, something she was certain that Edward would never do. Edward spends his time sitting by Bella's side as she completes homework or sleeps.

For young women like Andie, the average guy no longer suffices. In my interviewing, I heard variations of the same complaints: "Every boy that comes around that you would normally be interested in doesn't seem so great anymore," and, "It sorta sabotages my relationships." A parent at TwiCon explained to me that Edward is a Victorian gentleman who is different from twenty-first-century boys. Andie says that her mother invokes Edward whenever she broaches the topic of dating, urging her to look for Edward's qualities in potential boyfriends, the stalking notwithstanding. The Bella Cullen Project song "What's Wrong with Him?" talks about how the human boys, like Mike Newton at Bella's high school, don't know what chivalry is and urges Bella to "check out" Edward.

The guys who could speak in the language of Twilight, as both sensitive and strong, were destined for success with Twilight fans. A story in the *Twilight Guy* archives concerns a teenager named Eddie who meets a girl at a Halloween bash who is dressed as Bella, but in his Twilight ignorance, he assumes she'd just neglected to wear a costume. After the encounter, Eddie reads the series and is hooked by the story and the real "Bella." After a few dates, he writes, "As we were walking out, I figured now or never and asked Bella if she wouldn't mind being my stupid lamb. Ignoring her friends who awwed and cheered behind us, she just laughed and told me that she was glad it didn't take me 90 years." Male Twilight literacy could be the way to many of the fans' hearts. In the story, Eddie downloads Twilight love-note postcards culled from quotations in the book. "You smell so good in the rain" is the one that won over the girl dressed as Bella. Could it be that Twilight might have a dubious effect on a generation of boys growing up with the girl fans of Twilight? Could there be a new cadre of boys and men who will model themselves on Edward, thus multiplying the possibility that the girls may find their own romantic savior or stalker? Or in their embrace of Edward's emotional openness and sensitivity, they might prove to be exceptions to the kind of hypermasculinity, sense of sexual entitlement, and debauched behavior typical of many young men. Or they may assume that stalking a girl is acceptable as long as you truly love her.

Despite its traditional messages about girl power and the myth of true love, by virtue of being an almost all-female space, Twilight opens up possibilities for friendship, love, and intimacy for girls, unencumbered by guys. The young women in the aerobics and self-defense classes, listening to the Bella Cullen Project, eating together in the lobby, and gushing over the appearance of Kellan Lutz temporarily shed the pressures to compete for men, jobs, beauty, and achievement. It's not just an apolitical space of entertainment and consumption but also a potential moment of solidarity for lonely girls, popular girls, sporty girls, alternative girls, mean girls, and fat girls, one that revolves around shared tastes, preferences, and desires. Andie and Jenna; Hannah, Gabriella, Lara, and Diane; even the loner Carly and the Wichita women—they all spent their weekend at TwiCon delving into questions of what it meant to be a young woman and have a relationship through the workshops they attended or in the conversations they had, the kinds that are often impossible to have in the ordinariness of school, everyday friends, and their own communities. The promise of girl power here is that girls are figuring out collectively how to find their way through the choices that face them. They are also having a raucously good time.

At the evening vampire ball, the culminating event of TwiCon, Andie and Jenna bask in Twilight splendor. There is a buzz of excitement in the air as women enter the hall, which has been transformed into a ballroom with a giant illuminated Twilight sign, a stage, and hundreds of tables. With the exception of maybe a dozen men, it's like an all-female prom on steroids. Having spent a few hours consulting on their outfits and hair, as well as attending a dance class and mask-making workshop, Andie and Jenna enter in a sense of great anticipation. Andie appears in a frothy green dress and Converse sneakers in homage to Bella's outfit at her prom in the first Twilight movie, when her shattered leg forced her to wear sneakers. (In the book, Bella appears in stilettos with her cast, which, in my opinion, is one of the most supernatural moments of the entire series.) Others wear formal ball gowns with elaborate masks. The most grandiose are two women both dressed as Cinderella with enormous hoop skirts, corkscrew curls, masks, and their skin painted porcelain white. They can hardly move, much less dance in their ensembles, but that is irrelevant when the idea is to wait for their prince.

The DJ is whipping everyone into a frenzy of dancing, and the floor is actually vibrating. "I don't like blood, but I enjoy sucking on a few necks," he croons into the microphone. He tells revelers he's recently broken up with a girlfriend and had despaired of meeting anyone, but now he's feeling more hopeful. "Who lives in Dallas?" he asks. Some young women jump on stage to dance close to him, but security yanks them off. By chance, Hannah and Lara come by and ask me to guard their purses while they head to the dance floor. Andie says she hopes to dance with "an Edward," though the majority of attendees are women and girls. Jenna, homesick for Huntsville, wishes out loud that her boyfriend was here. Sighing, she and Jenna initially resign themselves to wallflower status, nibbling food set out at the tables. After about a half hour, when "Ice Ice Baby" comes on, in homage to Edward's cold beauty, they give up and rush to the dance floor, exuberantly bopping along to the music with thousands of other women.

⤛

On my way out of Dallas, I notice a young man in an army uniform in the security line at the airport, bidding farewell to his woefully stoic parents. He's carrying a faded-green duffel bag with a copy of *New Moon* and a pocket Bible poking out of it. Through fortune or fate, he sits in my row, so that even at 6 a.m., far from the hotel that hosted the TwiCon, I can't quite seem to escape Twilight. John is stationed in Korea until autumn, when he might end up back at Fort Hood or in Iraq. He's twenty but looks sixteen, with a slightly mischievous, goofy grin, and willingly admits he's read the Twilight series more than thirty times. At the base in Korea, he says, everyone has the books. At first, John claims, it was Emmett whom he identified with, for his strength and humor. But he came to admit that it's wasn't the vampire story that he enjoyed as much as the love story, which aligned with his Southern Baptist upbringing of finding the right person, getting married, and having eternal love. Sure, John's favorite scene is when Charlie, Bella's father, is cleaning his shotgun, but another favorite is when Bella reunites with Edward in the plaza of Volterra toward the end of *New Moon*, because, he says, you see that "they were meant to be together." The film of *New Moon* hadn't been released at the time of my conversation with John, but he and the other army recruits will watch a pirated version at the base, he says. It's strange and poignant to imagine Twilight's ideal of romance stretching from the convention halls of TwiCon across the sea to an army station in Korea.

CHEAT SHEET

Twilight

Bella Swan is plain and clumsy, but everyone in the small town of Forks, Washington, falls for her, including emo Edward Cullen, who wants to devour her because of her scent. Also, he can read minds, though not Bella's. He tries to stay away from her, but she is so irre-sistible to him that he creeps into her room at night and watches her sleep. They exchange smoldering glances across the crowded high school parking lot and cafeteria, and Bella endures a lot of "does he like me or hate me" turmoil.

Despite being the daughter of Charlie, the Forks police chief, Bella requires constant rescue. Edward saves her from being crushed by an errant van skidding on ice by pushing it out of the way one-handed. This is our first clue that Edward isn't your average high school guy. He also saves Bella from some would-be rapists who follow her down a dark and deserted street. (As someone once com-mented to me, in *Twilight*, whenever more than three human men are together, they tend to be rapists.)

Since we all know that the potential for murder and stalking is a terrific start to a relationship, Bella and Edward begin dating. Bella is immediately certain it is true love. Did I mention that Edward is a specimen of physical perfection and chivalry? Some of the ways Bella describes her beloved are angelic, perfect, a pagan god, bronze hair, gorgeous, a marble statue, golden, dazzling, topaz eyes, and, again, perfect. *Twitilating* is a fan term for that feeling you get whenever Edward looks more like a Greek god than anyone has a right to.

After a few days, Edward leads Bella to a meadow, where he takes off his shirt and reveals he is a vampire who sparkles in the sun.

> "And so the lion fell in love with the lamb . . .," he murmured. . . .
> I looked away, hiding my eyes as I thrilled to the word.
> "What a stupid lamb," I sighed.
> "What a sick, masochistic lion."

"Stupid Lamb" is a favorite slogan for fans to wear on t-shirts and pins.

Bella is dazzled by Edward's glittering body of perfection, but they don't kiss or attack each other with lust. They sprawl in a meadow strewn with purple flowers with their heads almost touching and stare longingly at each other. Edward insists on chastity because sex could quickly devolve into a Bella bloodbath. Also, having been a virgin for 107 years means that Edward's had a lot of time to practice abstinence.

In the film adaptation of *Twilight*, Edward almost winces when he kisses Bella, his pleasure and painful control intermingled. Just as things heat up in her bedroom and the bruising kiss turns hot and heavy, he hurls himself against a wall to make himself stop. Bella, hugging her coltish legs in her underwear, her lip quivering, looks confused. "I'm stronger than I thought," he tells her. Instead of having sex, they snuggle in her bed until she falls asleep with her head on his chest.

Edward's family, the vegetarian vampire Cullens, is also a paragon of vampire exquisiteness. Carlisle, the righteous doctor and patriarch, and his kind and lovely wife, Esme, are foster vamp parents to five teenagers who could be the vampire versions of high school archetypes: Rosalie, the popular, spoiled, blonde debutante; Emmett, the burly jock; Alice, the whimsical alternative girl with a flair for party planning and divining the future; and slightly geeky Jasper, a former soldier who can alter the moods of people around him. The Cullens begin to appear less glamorous and more supernaturally creepy in each consecutive film. Jasper wears an atrocious wiry wig, and Carlisle in particular is pasty and bloated.

Another character is Bella's friend Jacob Black, a member of the Quileute tribe who lives on the reservation, but he's not yet the bulked-up romantic rival of Edward, and his pre-werewolf transformation goofiness is endearing.

In *Twilight*, there is a vampire baseball game, a tracker vampire who hunts down Bella to her childhood dance studio, her deliverance by Edward again—and then there is prom. Bella wears a stunning dress with a giant cast on her leg because she was hurled against a wall of mirrors by an evil vampire. Edward and Bella sway dreamily in a gazebo. Bella wants him to turn her into a vampire. He leans his mouth toward her neck Dracula-style, but barely grazes her skin with his lips and asks her, "Isn't it enough to have a long happy life together?"

CHAPTER 2

Sparkle, You Fool, Sparkle!

Melissa wears a red spaghetti-strap gown with a black velvet shawl to attend the Forks High School prom. She enters the auditorium beneath the archway of balloons and sways to the music of the Mitch Hansen Band, a bluesy rock "Twi-band" whose song lyrics reflect the characters and themes of the four novels of the Twilight series. "By You" channels Bella's turmoil in *New Moon*, and "A World Without You" refers to Edward's lament and slow death from grief when he believes Bella has died. When a scowling young man dressed as Edward glides past with his partner, Melissa laughs nervously and sidles closer to the couple. Like many attendees, Melissa can quote verbatim from the Twilight books and competed in the Bella Swan Memorial Volleyball Tournament earlier that day in the high school gymnasium. These activities were part of Summer School in Forks, the weekend literary symposium for Twilight fans where I had met Rachel. As a member of the Newborns team (newly turned vampires), Melissa and dozens of other female fans flailed awkwardly on the court in their t-shirts with slogans like "I Can't Resist a Guy Who Sparkles." No one minded their ineptitude since Bella is clumsy and nonathletic. In fact, the Athletics section of our "yearbook," designed for the Twilight Summer School participants with pictures we had submitted, urged students to embrace their "inner klutz," informing them that "normally, volleyball is a game which requires balance, coordination and teamwork. But this is volleyball a la Bella where such skills not only aren't required, they are down-right discouraged."

During the Summer School weekend, Melissa ate in the high school cafeteria, inspected "Bella's" locker, and attended classes such as "Oh My, I'm in Love with a Vampire: What Makes *Twilight* Vamps Cool and Other Vamps Not." Yet Melissa, who happens to be forty-five years old, didn't stand out at prom, in the volleyball tournament, or among the throngs of fans rushing from one classroom to another. More than half of the students at the Summer School were women in their thirties and forties, and they were as ardent about Twilight as the thirteen-year-old girls.

Outsiders to the Twilight phenomenon can be forgiven for assuming that a middle-aged, married woman reliving her prom is a bit odd. After all, most of us would have to be dragged kicking and screaming back to the humiliation and tedium of our high school years. However, within the fanpire, it's a common refrain that Twilight evokes the giddiness and yearning of high school for adults. The news media have been less generous, disseminating stereotypes of adult fans as "stalker moms," pitiable addicts, and negligent parents.[1] One article described fanpire women this way: "It's not uncommon to hear them break into unprompted gasps, giggles, and squeals."[2] The implication is that these women just need to get a life instead of spending all their time obsessing about a frivolous interspecies romance. It may not help that "Edward Brings Out the Cougar in Me" is a popular t-shirt slogan for adult fans. Despite the derision in these caricatures of adult female fans, they point to an overlooked aspect of the Twilight phenomenon: Why *has* the series captured and captivated so many women? What desires does it speak to for adult women? And why does it make so many people uncomfortable that grown women are fervid fans?

The Twilight saga is, at heart, a text about romance embodied in marriage. The books reimagine marriage as passionate, committed, and secured with the guarantee of undying love. One woman at Summer School told me, "Edward and Bella aren't going to get in a fight and get divorced in ten years. They're going to be happy and love each other forever!" Bella is assured of eternity with the person she loves because, unlike humans, vampires are not fickle or transient. The centuries-long, impassioned marriage of Edward's adopted vampire parents, Esme and Carlisle, is proof of this ideal. The series fills the void left by the pervasive failure of mortal marriages to live up to the promises of romance, passion, and intimacy. From Christian theology to the genre of romance fiction, marriage has been portrayed as the inevitable and ideal culmination of romantic love.

As historians of marriage such as Stephanie Coontz have shown, the ideology of love is a recent innovation to a tradition that was formerly an economic transaction.[3] Today, the notion that heterosexual marriage epitomizes love in its highest form reigns supreme in the United States. One need only look at how the wedding business caters to many women's fantasies of princesses and fairytales.[4] But there is the damning evidence that the fantasy is not reality, not just in the high divorce rate in the United States, but in the ever-present rhetoric that marriage is also supposed to be "work" with its "ups and downs." Twilight presents the institution as something else: fulfilling, dangerous, and sublime.

Unlike the mundaneness of daily life, the books deliver the romantic goods with every read, which explains why so many fans devour the novels in one sitting or reread them twenty times. Given Twilight's idealization of a socioeconomic arrangement and the real-life drudgery of the marriages of most women, it's unsurprising that Melissa relishes the idea of going back in time, even to high school, to imagine different choices and possibilities she might have had. She explains: "A lot of us get married, have kids, and our husbands have busy jobs, things build and life gets so serious. It's hard to continue to have that romance of, 'I can't live without you.' It's just something that doesn't happen on a day-to-day basis when you have to take the kids to soccer practice, ballet, and make sure that they are up and dressed and fed and out the door and going to school at eight a.m."

I frequently see adult fans at Summer School and Twilight conventions wearing pins and t-shirts with the slogans "Sparkle, you fool, sparkle!" and "Edward ruined it for mortal men." These are worn partly as ironic statements, but the message of the pins and t-shirts also bespeaks a real sense of the failure of some marriages to satisfy women's longings for love and affinity. Marriage is at the core of the Twilight series, despite the fact that the books are labeled as young adult. And the relationships in the books are always heterosexual; there are no gay characters nor ever any indication that any other configuration outside of heterosexual monogamy might be satisfying and fulfilling, even though the saga attracts gay fans.[5]

Edward's condition for turning Bella into a vampire is that she marry him first. His rationale is that he's old-fashioned, but he also doubts whether he has a soul and believes marriage is the only proper way to seal his relationship with Bella before she becomes immortal. Also, it's the virtuous thing to do. As Edward says in *Eclipse*: "You know that I've stolen, I've lied, I've coveted . . . my virtue is all I have left." Bella is initially more horrified at the idea of being an eighteen-year-old bride than she is by becoming a vampire, and it is a source of constant tension. She says to Edward, "Do you realize what century this is? People don't just get married at eighteen! Not smart people, not responsible, mature people!" When Bella decides she wants to experience sex with him as a human, Edward agrees, despite his reservations about injuring her due to his supernatural strength. However, he will only attempt it after they are properly married. Later, she relents and, at the end of *Eclipse*, must even reconvince Edward of his proposal when he suddenly attempts to ravish her in a meadow.

Marriage represents tradition in the books, and the only moral and ethical way to live: Edward declares that the day he places an engagement ring on Bella's finger is the best day of his century-long life. The unspoken expectation of Twilight is that all normal people have partners, and if you don't have a mate of the opposite sex, you aren't a whole person. The bonds of matrimony are eternal and sacred, reflecting, as I note elsewhere, the Mormon theology of marriage as an experience that transcends the earthly realm. This idea is particularly salient for fans, many of whom identify as non-denominational Christians or as members of the LDS Church, including author Stephenie Meyer as well as Lisa Hansen, the founder of *TwilightMoms*.

This idea of the sanctity of marriage finds an even more extreme expression in the behavior of Jacob and his fellow members of the Quileute wolf pack. The wolves, like the vampires, are committed monogamists, but instead of eternal marriage, they undergo a biological process called imprinting in which they bond for life with selected females. One day you're just a burly Quileute shape-shifter, and the next you adore one woman for the rest of your life. Jacob imprints upon Renesmee, the daughter of Edward and Bella, when she is merely a toddler, bestowing upon her the equivalent of a promise ring. Note that the woman is always the passive recipient of imprinting, and she cannot refuse to be imprinted.

How have adult women engaged with Twilight's picture of marriage as awash with a dangerous sense of romance, yet also as ethical, eternal, and sacred? To figure it out, in 2009, I attended a weekend-long celebration of the *New Moon* film premiere in Salt Lake City with four thousand other adult fans. Members of *Twilight-Moms*, one of the largest and only fan sites limited exclusively to adult women, had formed an event-planning organization, Events by Alice, named for Edward's sister Alice, who cajoles Bella into allowing her to organize her birthday party, graduation celebration, and even wedding. The impetus for the *New Moon* event was to support Alex's Lemonade Stand, a national charity dedicated to raising money for treatment of and research on childhood cancer. Many organizations hold lemonade-stand events in memory of Alex, a young girl who died of pediatric cancer.

The *New Moon* event is also meant to capitalize on the massive fan base for the Twilight series in Utah (one estimate is that over 90 percent of Mormon women have read the books, and that 45 percent of the audience for the first Twilight movie was women over age twenty-five.)[6] To accommodate everyone, Events by Alice reserved eight Salt Lake City movie theaters for midnight screenings at a megaplex and nearby convention center. The women running the event, predominantly members of the LDS Church, had all volunteered. For the premiere, they painstakingly recreated scenes from *New Moon* in a cavernous convention center where attendees enjoyed the festivities before seeing the film.

Because I Read Twilight
I Have Unrealistic Expectations of Men

In the convention hall, there was talk of the exceptional ideal of Edward Cullen and then the rest of mankind, who more closely resembled Bella's hunting, beer-drinking, emotionally absent father, Charlie. I heard descriptions of Edward as attentive, a gentleman, and a throwback to another era (when presumably men treated women better and were self-deprecating and protective). And not only does Edward possess eyes of "liquid gold" (*Eclipse*) whose gaze could make Bella light-headed and "a face any male model in the world would trade his soul for," he also announces his feelings with a combination of romantic metaphor and smoldering innuendo:

> Before you, Bella, my life was like a moonless night, very dark, but there were stars—points of light and reason. . . . And then you shot across my sky like a meteor. Suddenly everything was on fire; there was brilliancy, there was beauty.

He also tells her, in the first Twilight film, "You are utterly indecent—no one should look so tempting, it's not fair." After a long day, the idea of experiencing liquid eyes and being compared to a meteor was immensely appealing to the women in the convention hall.

Jessica, acting director of Events by Alice, was willingly offering a refresher course on romance for men:

> Open the door for a girl, let her know that you think she's the most beautiful thing you have ever seen. Give her a flower unexpectedly, touch her hair. She buys that certain kind of conditioner because she likes the smell. She wants to be recognized, and you can stop for two seconds in your life and say, "Oh you look nice." If they could pause and take those lessons, it's guaranteed the woman they are with, the wife they have, the girlfriend that they have, [she] would be satisfied.

Many women at the premiere commented that Edward never disappoints, unlike some oblivious husbands to whom they've been married for ten or twenty years. The event presumed that all women were saddled with good but inattentive men like Charlie, who were oblivious to perfume and poetry, much less declarations of love and meteors.

Despite the supernatural aspects of the books, the set-up of the convention hall, the site of the pre-screening festivities, promoted the idea that most men prefer sports, hunting, and motorcycles to romantic vampires and the women they love. "Charlie's living room," occupying an entire corner of the hall, was an exact replica of the place where Bella's father watches sports on TV in a Barcalounger. The organizers had included small touches like his hunting rifle and favorite brand of beer resting next to the couch. Another scene featured a motorcycle and a rack with various greasy tools for fixing bikes in homage to Jacob Black's garage. If any husband had accompanied his spouse to the event, these spaces were meant to ease his discomfort with the more feminine aspects of the Twilight saga.

The women in Utah talked as if the men in their lives were less Edward and more Charlie, a man too zoned out on fishing and watching football to notice that his daughter is dating a vampire and, later, becoming one. In *New Moon*, even when Bella experiences what she calls the worst night of her life, sobbing in her room until dawn because Edward has dumped her, she knows Charlie won't disturb her because of his "fear of emotional outbursts." He's harmless and hapless, easily distracted and manipulated. What is lacking in these women's marriages is much simpler than a deficiency of poetry or chivalry: there seems to be sometimes a scarcity of communication and support.

Tracie Lamb, writing in a special issue of *Sunstone,* a progressive Mormon journal, explains that Twilight delivers to women what they may lack from husbands: rapt attention, strong protection, and total devotion.[7] In *Twilight*, Bella recalls spending time with Edward like this: "I couldn't remember the last time I'd talked so much. . . . But the absolute absorption of his face, and his never-ending stream of questions, compelled me to continue." Of course, not all men are inept conversationalists, but the consensus of the women I met was that some were prone to talk only about themselves and were clueless about romance. Lamb writes, "Edward is the romance master, guys. Learn from him."

Paige, in her early thirties and dressed in retro-1940s vintage heels with her hair pinned up and wearing bright-red lipstick, was the only divorced woman I spoke with at the convention hall. Her criterion for romance had been downgraded to finding someone emotionally supportive who would stick around if things weren't going well, like losing a job or having a miscarriage.

In a few exceptional cases, there was the man who wholeheartedly embraced the Edward archetype, intent on rekindling romance from its neglect. Kim, a self-effacing thirty-year-old with freckles and ponytailed hair, was responsible for the impressive array of crafts for sale. Her husband delighted in Twilight and even listened to all the books on CD. In August 2009, Kim secretly packed his suitcase, rented him a tuxedo, and recruited a friend to drive him to the airport where she surprised him with a ticket to Dallas for the three-day TwiCon convention that I had attended. He gamely accompanied her to the Saturday night vampire ball and various *TwilightMoms* special events like an exclusive dinner with some of the film's actors. Even he had his limits, though. One night as they lay in their bed with a giant framed poster of Edward (or, rather, Robert Pattinson, the brooding actor who portrays Edward in the films) over them, he jumped up, tore it off the wall, and hid it in the closet. "That's it," he said. "Edward's not watching us sleep anymore." ("Watch Me Sleep, Edward" is a popular slogan on fan t-shirts in reference to the fact that Edward slips into Bella's room at night without her knowing.)

One man in his mid-thirties from Utah keeps a blog entitled *Normal Mormon Husband*, where he bemoans the fact that so many LDS women, including his wife of twelve years, have read the books and hanker for a husband like Edward or Jacob. The popularity of the sticker that reads, "I like my men cold, dead and sparkling," indicates the prevalence of this sentiment. Dispensing Twilight wisdom for "dummies and guys," he provides quotes for men to use if they haven't read the books but want to sound as if they have. "If she thinks that you drive too recklessly: 'Honey, please trust me as much as Bella trusted Edward when he had to break all known traffic laws to get her out of Forks and away from Victoria. If he can drive Bella's pickup truck that recklessly, then I should be able to steer with my knees while texting with my right hand and using my left hand to hold my Slurpee.'" When a woman says she's cold, he responds, "My body always feels cold to the touch . . . kind of like Edward's." "You can then raise your eyebrows like *Magnum, P.I.*, flex your pecs, and put your arm around her," he advises. Finally, he urges married men to showcase their bonds of eternal marriage as members of the Church in an anniversary card that reads, "I am eternally grateful to know that we can be together forever. I am even more grateful that I did not have to sink my vampire teeth into your neck and suck out all of your blood to make it happen." Rather than seriously emulating Edward, he tells his readers, "Edward is just as flawed as the rest of us guys out there. Ladies, you can look all you want and you will never find perfection in a man."

Even Edward can't live up the ideal of Edward. There was an Edward impersonator, the son of a volunteer, with a boyish, pallid face mingling with women in the hall. Attendees could corral him into one of the photo booths featuring backgrounds of scenes from the film, if you could get to him amid the competition. Earlier, I'd met two women who gushed that they had dragged the Edward impersonator into the booth with them as they clutched ten photos as prizes. I had noticed the fake Edward become increasingly standoffish and grumpy as the night progressed, and, at one point, the crisis for Jessica and the other organizers was that he was missing in action, much to his mother's chagrin.

Addicted to Romance

If one premise of the weekend was that there were only a smattering of men willing to transform themselves from Charlie to Edward, the other premise was that women could inject some liveliness into dismal marriages and entice their husbands out of that Barcalounger.

Rather than questioning gender dynamics, the convention's activities implied that women would become worthy of the love of someone comparable to Edward, or even someone who might stick by during a job loss or miscarriage, through personal upkeep and remodeling. For my attendance fee of $25, I was eligible for three homemade cupcakes, a manicure or hairstyling session, a sparkling apple tattoo, a t-shirt that flickers from white to maroon in the sunlight with the promise that it accentuates your "assets," and my movie ticket. So many women lined up to have their hair curled and styled with hot irons by students from the beauty college down the road that they all began to bear an uncanny resemblance to each other. Regardless of age, everyone's hair featured the loose cascading ringlets that Bella wears to her prom in the *Twilight* film or the sleek coiffure worn at her birthday soiree at the beginning of *New Moon*. One booth was selling various types of corsets. Like the Bella hairstyle, the body molds might perfect and shape us. And if that didn't work, there was the solace of cupcakes.

Paige told me, "When I read these books, and I feel these emotions, it reminds me of what it was like to be so in love with somebody that you just couldn't breathe unless they were standing right next to you." Immersion in the books is inexplicable, heady, irresponsible, consuming, and even draining. It's as if women are enmeshed in an adulterous affair with a paramour who just happens to be a character in a book—and in their imaginations. Reading these books is not a cerebral experience but a deeply emotional and physical one, in which the readers live vicariously through the narration, like a somatic PG experience of torrid romance.

It's not just captivation with Edward; the real affair adult fans are having is with themselves. They see their younger, optimistic, and risk-taking selves mirrored back to them in the books. It's certainly escapism, but it also returns fans to a time when they could envision themselves outside of the label of mother or wife. Women succumb to long-buried feelings and share intimacies with other women at these Twilight events. Prom, all-women sleepovers, and weekend-long conventions are a titillating break from ordinary time and space. *TwilightMoms* founder Lisa Hansen tells me, "The books reawakened those emotions I had not experienced in so long. It was a reminder of who I really am, and I have noticed a lot of women have had that same feeling. I think it was just basically— The book was able to tap into that part that had just gone off to the side for so long."

Paige recounted a rowdy night at a fellow *TwilightMoms* member's house with about twenty other women. They weren't drinking or carousing but staying up all night playing Twilight trivia games, sharing confidences, and weeping. Kim cried as she recalls that first event. "We just bonded," she says. "We just sat and talked for hours and hours. We didn't even— None of us knew anybody, and it wasn't until three in the morning that we finally sat around on the couches and introduced ourselves." There is a nascent vein of repression and release here. In online forums where TwiMoms complain and rant, in sleepovers, in the gyrations and screaming to music of Mitch Hansen (no relation to Lisa Hansen), and even in their reactions to the film, a dormant well of emotions and desires erupts. Jessica confides, "I have been married for fourteen years now, and I have five children. And for so long you are there for someone else all the time. There is not a moment in your day or night that you are not on-call for someone else's needs."

Jessica, along with Kim and others, had attended *TwilightMoms* sleepover events. "I mean, come on, if you're an older lady, when was the last time you were at a slumber party?" she says. In those all-night sessions, they revert to the flushed intimacies of adolescence, and they also hash out problems about husbands, marriages, and children and the dissatisfaction in their lives. After a few of these sleepovers, Paige and Kim organized a trip to Forks for 250 Twilight-Moms. Paige made a commemorative t-shirt: "Airfare: $250, Hotel: $400, Getting to travel with your Internet friends to a fictional place in reality: Priceless."

Rather than dubbing these moments of hysteria or adolescent folly, adult women's emotional responses to Twilight are an indication that they're seizing something invigorating and emotionally cathartic from Twilight that is absent from the rest of their lives. Many women fixate on Bella's trauma in *New Moon*. After Edward leaves her, she awakens night after night screaming and clutching the sheets. "How many of us, when we have a hard time, just want to scream in our bed every single night, just scream. But, you know, we're the mom. We don't want to scare our kids so we don't," Kim tells me.

The pervasive narrative about adult Twilight fans is that they are frivolous and addicted to a pleasurable experience that radically departs from the everyday comportment they're expected to exhibit as wives and mothers. The *Los Angeles Times* ran a piece about the irresponsible, out-of-control behavior of adult women entitled "When 'Twilight' Fandom Becomes Addiction: Some Fans of the Book and Film Series Are Finding Their Obsession Is Hurting Other Parts of Their Lives."[8] *TwilightMoms* devotes a multitude of message threads to the issue of whether Twilight is frivolous and addictive, and on fan sites like *TwiCrackAddict*, *Twilighters Anonymous*, and *Cullen Boys Anonymous*, fans disavow their Twilight fixation even while they embrace it with differing degrees of sincerity and playfulness. Jessica said that her husband thinks the book pages are laced with cocaine because they are so impossible to put down.

The *Los Angeles Times* article and others like it tend to focus on the exceptional adult fanatic. Although there are women who are clearly obsessed with Twilight, these media representations are themselves a form of hysteria or an indicator of a broader anxiety about adult women. Why not equal concern for men (and some women) overtaken by Star Trek or the NCAA basketball playoffs? Is there an implicit panic that these women might become so enmeshed in Twilight and disenchanted with the state of their marriages that they will discard the idea of marriage itself? Like penitents at confession, contributors to *TwilightMoms* often relate various versions of the same story: banishing children to the backyard in order to watch the Twilight films or read the books over and over, spending too much time in fan forums, and daydreaming about their favorite characters while disgruntled husbands seethed. Paige watched the first film five times in twenty-four hours, but this time around, with the coming of the second film, she's "gained a little bit of sanity." Jessica recalls when "dinner did not get made and the laundry did not get done" until she told herself: "Oh, my gosh, why I am doing this? This is ridiculous. I shouldn't be so addicted."

If every story I heard from *TwilightMoms* was true, then a lot of children out there were eating bowls of cold cereal for dinner. At the same time, there was self-policing in the women's stories. They had internalized the criticism that this breach of behavior is acceptable as long as women acknowledge it is temporary. So, the forums feature equal numbers of testimonies from women who attest to a recovery from their bouts of romantic mania as they do testimonies of obsession. These comeback narratives are everywhere in the forums: "I think I'm kind of like not necessarily over it, but I've reached a healthy maturity. I can appreciate this, but I don't necessarily need everything *Twilight*," wrote one contributor to a forum I read. Or as Jessica relates, "I've found that being able to just walk away from the computer, to turn it off . . . restores some balance and I can focus on my kids."

The Hand That Rocks the Cradle

The impetus for *TwilightMoms* emerged from a lonely mother's enthrallment with Twilight. Lisa Hansen, thirty-nine with long curly hair and an air of busy glamour about her, initially started *Twilight-Moms* in her Utah home. Her sixteen-year-old neighbor, Lauren, pestered Lisa constantly about reading *Twilight* until Lisa finally caved in and borrowed the book. After ripping through it in one night, she called Lauren frantic for a copy of *New Moon,* but Lauren was out. Lisa harassed Lauren's mother, asking her in vain to search Lauren's room for it or call her at the movies. Finally, in desperation, she drove to the nearest bookstore and bought a copy for herself. Once home, Lisa shooed her children outside and started reading. "And it completely turned my life upside down," she says with a laugh.

In a desperate search for other thirty-something women who shared her obsession, Lisa decided to create a website on the subject and taught herself how to do it late at night while her children were sleeping. In some ways, Lisa's narrative mirrors that of Stephenie Meyer, who sacrificed her nights and evenings to write the Twilight series. As soon as Lisa finished designing her site, she logged on to look at Stephenie Meyer's official website but was disappointed to find that other fan sites were overwhelmingly helmed by teenagers. Lisa longed for a peer, someone at her stage of life who might have a different perspective on the books. "I was getting discouraged and starting to wonder if I was going through a midlife crisis or something," she tells me. Through her website and forums, Lisa is now connected to the more than ten thousand other *TwilightMoms* all over the world. Their tagline is "The Hand That Rocks the Cradle Is the Hand That Rules the World."

To be fair, even if there is simmering discontent, guilt, and even mild addiction among visitors to the *TwilightMoms* forums, there was no shortage of frivolity and joy throughout the weekend. During my two days of *New Moon* build-up at the convention hall in Utah, I watched people cheering for women in the muffin-eating contest enticed by the tagline "Think you can beat Paul in wolfing down Emily's famous blueberry muffins? Come challenge other guests." Unlike some of the corporate Twilight conventions, there was an entrepreneurial, DIY vibe here. Each item for sale had been made by a local business or individual: Twilight-themed paintings and sculpture, jewelry, homemade t-shirts, and even aprons with slogans like "Cooking for the Wolf Pack" as a nod to Emily, who selflessly bakes for the ravenous werewolves after they've been pounding through the forest chasing vampires. There were also quilts intricately stitched with scenes from the books and five-tiered cakes with miniature vampire and werewolf figurines on each layer. Around me, fans played Twilight-bingo and assembled for the costume contest later that afternoon. Even if I didn't want Bella's curls or a corset, I couldn't be a killjoy amid the infectious camaraderie pervading the convention hall. I waited with everyone else for my free manicure and marveled at the polish, which sparkled in the sun. I even congratulated myself when I correctly answered the question about how Jacob initially feels about becoming a shape-shifting wolf posed to me by a "traveling trivia trickster," a roaming volunteer whose job it was to hand out prizes for correct responses.

Paige tells me that being a part of *TwilightMoms* means she can call anyone in her broad community of friends and talk about a specific passage or ask if they had bought the pair of Twilight-themed earrings. "You feed off of each other and you need that connection," she says. "It's a sisterhood of friends who accept you for who you are. *Twilight* was the catch, but now it has gone so far beyond *Twilight*. It is a group of women that are bonded on so many different levels." Kim traveled outside Utah for the first time in her life to Dallas, Forks, and to Comic-Con in Los Angeles for Twilight events. Her most intimate relationships are with women she met through these trips, and although they live in Baltimore and Washington State, they arrange to meet every six months at a Twilight event. As a way of being romantic with each other, members of *TwilightMoms* have a shared ritual of sending each other cards and gifts when no one else in their lives remembers to do it. What was romantic about Twilight was the headiness of immersion in the stories, the friendships engendered by the shared obsession, and, if not the possible resuscitation of these women's marriages, at least the possibility of it.

The women might be disillusioned by what had been promised to them in marriage or collectively revved up by the *New Moon* event, but it wasn't as if Twilight caused them to want to question marriage or overthrow the institution itself. In her article "The End of Men," Hanna Rosin argues that women are getting ahead now more than ever, with exponential increases in power in their jobs, education, and careers. Rosin notes that women are outperforming men in schools and work, while in the global economy, jobs that favor "female" characteristics, like nursing, are on the rise. At the same time, male-dominated industries such as manufacturing, construction, and finance are declining. What if, Rosin asks, "the economics of the new era are better suited to women?" Other new books bemoan a reverse gender gap in which young single women outearn men and female breadwinners must renegotiate gender roles at home.[9]

However, when it comes to women's economic achievement, the facts still speak otherwise. Many of the fastest-growing, female-dominated industries do not require a college education and are among the lowest paid. As of 2007, the top five jobs for women were, in order, secretaries, registered nurses, elementary and middle schoolteachers, cashiers, and retail salespeople. And though there are a handful of female CEOs and US senators, women have yet to crack the glass ceiling in any significant numbers.[10] Catalyst, a nonprofit that examines women in business, published a report that said women in corporate positions made no significant gains in 2011 and are doing no better than they were six years ago.[11] Yes, female college graduates told Hanna Rosin they hoped to become surgeons *and* marry men who would be their children's primary caregivers, but research shows that few women actually realize this domestic arrangement. They tend to marry high-achieving men who expect their own careers to take precedence.[12] As Irin Carmon writes in *Salon*, there is a "dissonance between the mostly grim headlines about American women's progress and the mild hand-wringing of the women-on-top school."[13]

Articles like Rosin's promote the postfeminist idea that feminism has made such massive gains and that women have achieved more than parity that we no longer have to confront the realities of parental-leave policies, wage gaps, and other barriers to workplace equality. Carmon sarcastically and accurate dubs this notion of a "wild feminist hegemony" a fallacy. The lack of a fair parental-leave policy in the United States, the astronomical cost of child care, and the fact that most women still find achieving a work-and-family balance untenable are not mentioned in these articles. Susan Douglas hauntingly illustrates this conundrum at the end of her book *Enlightened Sexism*, when she shows how her daughter must choose between hiring someone to take care of her children or quit her high-paying, satisfying job as a lawyer and do it herself.[14] Douglas offers an alternative vision of a world where her daughter's firm has a federally funded child-care center on site, flexible work hours and work sharing, generous maternity leave, and other family support services. The way things are now, that scenario is more fantastical than that of a vampire sweeping you off your feet.

For me, the romance of Twilight's version of marriage isn't necessarily Edward's sappy proclamations of love but the other dazzling possibilities in the text: the vampires don't eat actual food, so Bella is liberated from ever having to cook a meal or clean up once she becomes immortal. She eventually lives as part of an extended clan of Cullen vampires who are always on call to babysit and provide free day care. Sex is always awesome. And then there is immortality itself. However, these weren't the characteristics the women I spoke to found compelling. After working on the Utah event all day, Jessica was most concerned about returning home at night in time to do the laundry and clean the house. Even when Stephenie Meyer answered questions on *TwilightMoms*, the thing most readers asked her about was whether she hired a housekeeper or did the cleaning herself. For readers of *TwilightMoms*, Meyer embodies the quintessential mother and wife, just like them. Hansen says, "Moms have these fantasies of their house being completely clean all the time. We just ask [Stephenie Meyer] silly questions like that. I thought it was really fun to just get to know her basically, and she was one of us. Just like anybody, any friend you would meet." She just happens to be a millionaire.

These women wouldn't be forming all-women Twilight fan compounds with shared child care, but there were tentative critiques of the saga's vision of relationships for girls at the *New Moon* event. At one point during the weekend, I spoke to Tracy, a young mother of five whose cheerful weariness was palpable when we sat on a platform that held the Volterra clock tower, another set piece designed to emblemize a climactic moment in the book. She heaved a sigh after chasing her daughter, who has Down syndrome, around the room. In front of the tower, as part of the day's entertainment, a woman whirled in an interpretive dance to the theme music from the film. At the end of the piece, she slid gracefully downward and collapsed on the floor in a heap. It was the gestural equivalent of Bella crumpling into a ball in the forest behind her home, devastated and hopeless after Edward tells her he's leaving her.

As we sit with her nine year old, Tracy watches the dancer with distaste and scorn. "Yeah, relationships can hurt, they can, but you can't just die," she says. "You have to pull yourself up." She elaborates that Bella is a terrible role model because she bases "her value, on whether or not this guy likes her or that he's going to stick around." I heard other versions of this criticism as well, but it did not keep women from attending nor Tracy from volunteering hundreds of hours for the event. Perhaps it meant that someday she might have a conversation with her daughter about what the books reflect about relationships.

The gulf between the Twilight fantasy and the evident inadequacy of real married life doesn't inspire visions of gender equitable romance. Instead, the real-life romances engendered by the books are about friendships and alliance. The saga is a comfort for these women because it doesn't challenge what many of them have already chosen: a version of the Barcalounger husband who can't cook pasta. Kim puts it this way, "It helps us remember why we are where we're at. Why we got married, why we have kids, and why we want to continue to love them like that forever." Twilight valorizes the choices of traditional marriage and motherhood, the same choices so many fans have already made, while cloaking them in a veneer of supernatural romance. Even while women project themselves into the fantasy of Bella, what is mesmerizing is that as the romance and passion unfold, the fans know that these characters, desperately in love, held apart by their human and vampire differences ultimately end up like a heterosexual married couple with children. By the end of *Breaking Dawn*, the final book in the series, Bella and Edward lay awake at night, worrying about and bickering over their daughter just like parents everywhere. The transition from adolescent ardor to domesticity is seamless. The real fantasy and romance of Twilight for adult women is that it tells them the everyday, ordinary world of marriage they inhabit is the only way to live.

If I wanted any further confirmation of this, all I had to do was watch the fans' reactions to the midnight screening of *New Moon*. After the ballroom dancing, the muffin-eating, the trivia, the 10 p.m. bingo contest with an annoying number of questions focused on Charlie's eating habits and Bella's relentless litany of what she cooks for him ("What is Charlie's favorite meal?"), it's finally time to start assembling for the culminating event, the midnight movie premiere. I sympathize with the apparent collective flagging of energy and wonder how I'll manage to stay awake myself. Desperate times require desperate measures, so I cash in the cupcake portion of my entrance ticket, hoping that a sugar boost might buoy me. I've already eaten two cupcakes and, despite the array of aprons for sale, there is no other substantial food to be had at the entire event. Across the vast strip-mall parking lot, the megaplex beckons with lurid neon purple and green lighting. When I manage to force my way inside the lobby, it's a mob scene with tangled lines for the theater and the concession stand snaking out of the door. The people in line jostling, eating popcorn, and slightly breathless with anticipation are mainly adult women. Members of Events by Alice in red t-shirts herd us into one of the several theaters at the megaplex showing the film. Inside, the room hums with women laughing excitedly and chatting.

The lights dim and the previews begin, but no one is paying much attention until the opening credits appear, and then the theater is engulfed in a giant roar. The applause, yelling, and crying don't abate for almost two hours. When Jacob first appears shirtless with his newly chiseled, body-builder physique, mopping the blood from Bella's forehead after she crashes on a motorcycle, the theater reverberates with a collective swoon. When Jacob, relentlessly trying to convince Bella to see him as more than a friend, says, "You like me, right?" A woman yells, "I do!" to the sounds of hilarity. However, after a film rife with emotional breakdowns, cliff-diving, motorcycle accidents, shirtless vampires and werewolves, vampire-on-vampire violence, renewed vows of love, and a thwarted Romeo and Juliet scenario, what is it that elicits the collective sigh, a great many tears, wild clapping, and becomes the endless subject of post-film chatter for week? The last line of the film when Edward implores Bella: "Marry me."

CHEAT SHEET

New Moon

As Bella turns eighteen, she is freaking out because she's certain that while she'll grow up to become a wrinkled old crone, the immortal Edward will always remain a perfect, marble, dazzling vampire. At Bella's birthday party, Jasper, still acclimating to a non-human diet, attacks her, and as Carlisle Cullen, Edward's father, bandages her wound, Carlisle admits that he's damned for being a vampire, even one who abstains from drinking the blood of other humans. Edward won't turn Bella into a vampire because he doesn't want to risk taking away her soul.

The next morning, Edward and Bella rendezvous in the woods, where he informs her that his family is leaving Forks and that he'll never see her again. This is somewhat confusing to Bella since the night before Edward told her, "You give me everything just by breathing." He had also declared, "You are my life now." Because she's perennially insecure, Bella accepts his rejection pitifully: "You don't want me?" "No," Edward tells her and vanishes. The only thing Bella can think to do is curl up in the fetal position right there in the forest to die or at least get hypothermia. However, she is Bella and, therefore, is carried from the woods by Sam Uley of the Quileute wolf pack.

What should you do when your boyfriend dumps you? Bella spends the next six months moping in her room, awaking at night screaming from nightmares, and endangering herself by riding motorcycles and approaching groups of semidrunk men outside bars so she'll hear Edward's voice, chastising her for not being careful.

Now her solace is Jacob, his hair shorn and his body rippling with muscles, who effortlessly climbs through her bedroom window as Edward did. Bella spends as much time with Jacob as she did with Edward, and her high school friends are quickly cast aside. Jacob is part of a pack of Quileute werewolves whose sworn enemies are vampires, so when bad vampires continue to attempt to kill Bella, Jake, her new savior, and his pack fight them off. The wolves can hear each other's thoughts, so they bicker a lot, morph into wolves when someone insults them, and eat a lot of muffins cooked by Emily, their default caretaker who is also the fiancée of Sam, the alpha wolf. One of the wolf pack says of Bella, "This chick runs with vampires."

For all the threats she receives from vampires and werewolves, it's actually Bella who hurts herself. She dives off a cliff in another maudlin attempt to hear Edward's voice chastising her. Thinking she's died, Edward—whom we know will try to kill himself because there has been a lot of foreshadowing with his and Bella's reading of *Romeo and Juliet* in English class—does just that. Since poison doesn't work on vampires, Edward's method of suicide consists of provoking the Volturi, the vampire aristocracy who live in Italy, into killing him. How? By exposing his glittery chest to a crowd, thus breaking a cardinal vampire rule to keep his body concealed from humans. Bella and Alice, Edward's sister, rush to Italy to save Edward (in the film, she flies on Virgin Air) and narrowly escape the Volturi's grip before the Volturi massacre a group of unsuspecting tourists.

Back in Forks, Edward and Bella resume declaring their undying love to one another. "I couldn't live in a world where you don't exist," he tells her. Bella's response: "I'm nothing. It doesn't make sense for you to love me." She adds, "No matter how much more special or beautiful or brilliant or perfect than me he might be . . . I would always belong to him."

The takeaways here for girls are that, even if someone breaks up with you and leaves you, he doesn't mean it, and if you almost destroy yourself, he'll come back and ask you to marry him.

CHAPTER 3

Families That Prey
Together, Stay Together

They've flown from Maryland to Seattle, and driven more than four hours to arrive in damp, rainy, and remote Forks in time for Bella's engagement party. It is the kick-off event for Stephenie Meyer Day weekend, the fifth annual celebration of the Twilight saga's author and the birthday of her fragile and contentious creation, Bella Cullen, born September 13.

The idea of the weekend is to thank Meyer, who, without ever visiting Forks until the first book of the series was already on press, used the Internet to choose Forks as the setting for the series. No one realized Twilight's success would transform Forks into a tourist destination and repository for fans' longings for the otherworldly. A motel sign reading, "Edward slept here" greets visitors, an inside joke for Twilight fans since it's known that Edward Cullen, unlike most other light-averse vampires, doesn't need to sleep.

Gawky and shy, Gwen, sixteen, brushes her heavy black bangs from her eyes as she speaks, and her braces glint when she makes an occasional sly remark about forty-two-year-old Susan, her blond and vivacious Twilight-smitten mother. Gwen has good-naturedly traipsed to Forks from Maryland with Susan, and her patient tolerance of the event contrasts with her mom's ebullience, making it appear that they've swapped parental roles. Gwen entered her early teen years as the Twilight phenomenon gathered momentum, and she has passed through them with her mom beside her. They're devoted fans and acolytes: securing front-row seats at conventions, calling each

52

other throughout the day to share breaking news and gossip, camping in a tent city for days for the *Breaking Dawn* premiere, and now making the pilgrimage to Forks, the ultimate fan destination. They've branded themselves "Twibond," and Susan spends hours updating their Facebook page, where she emphasizes bonding within families and with other fans over Twilight. Susan and Gwen are plotting how to create a unique blog in an online universe littered with thousands of fan sites. The twibonding in the fandom of Twilight will be their hook. "It's Monday. What Twilight bond have you made today?" they ask on their Facebook page. Gwen's brother, a college student with minimal interest in Twilight, even accompanied his mother and sister to a Comic-Con in San Diego, serving as their support person by ferrying water and snacks back and forth from his hotel room to the ever-present lines to see the Twilight actors' panel. Before Susan discovered the local chapter of *TwilightMoms*, her social life revolved around Twilight activities with just her daughter, Gwen. At one point, Susan realized, "I need friends besides my fourteen-year-old."

But now they are on their way to the Stephenie Meyer weekend. As the road dips and swoops toward Forks, Gwen shakily aims their video camera out the window at the tattered landscape of denuded hills wrought by the local lumber industry punctuated by snow-capped peaks. Forks, population 3,175, including "8.5 vampires," according to one sign, has been swept up in Twilight mania and invaded by pilgrims like Gwen and Susan, eager to experience firsthand the novels' setting. As one woman who drove all night and slept in the Forks high school parking lot in her car tells me, "Every *true* Twilight fan needs to make their pilgrimage to Mecca, aka Forks."

At a time in life when parent-child relationships tend to be the most contentious, Susan and Gwen are not adversaries but rather coconspirators in a mutual pop-culture obsession. As Susan headed to the bathroom in the Baltimore airport, she jauntily called out to Gwen Edward's line from *Eclipse*, "I'll be back so soon you won't have time to miss me," as Gwen giggled. The two manage to discuss sex, boys, and Susan's divorce from Gwen's father through the safety and remove of Twilight's plot twists and characters. Gwen is utterly indifferent to dating. She calls herself an "old soul." She isn't obsessing about the boys in her high school or fighting her mom about curfews, and she finds the idea of sex repellant and scary. She tells me she flinched and covered her eyes watching an episode of HBO's provocative series *True Blood*.

I met countless fan families like that of Gwen and Susan. There is the mother and her fifteen-year-old daughter from Southern California who obstinately refuses to read anything else because she wants to devote all her time to Twilight and other books, she says, would make her feel disloyal. There's the self-designated Twilight Dad, a forty-seven-year-old former naval officer with swept-back bleached-white hair and pale skin made up to resemble Dr. Carlisle Cullen. The Twilight Dad attends fan events with his thirteen-year-old daughter wearing matching vampire contact lenses. There's the girl from Oregon whose mother surprised her by decorating her bedroom as a Twilight haven: walls painted red, black, and white; Bella's purple flowered bedspread; posters of Cullens on the wall; and black-and-white-painted shelves filled with Twilight paraphernalia. And then there's the family with the Twilight shrine in their home: two eight-foot-long, glass display cabinets overflowing with objects such as vampire wine bottles, Indian masks, a white chess piece, a worn bumper sticker that reads "Smitten," "I Kissed a Werewolf" shot glasses, tampons (to invoke blood), beads, and wolf figurines.

Notwithstanding the retrograde messages about violence, fated love, possessive men, and waffling girls, the books have the perhaps unintended consequence of enabling some families to help their daughters cross the chasm between childhood and adulthood more gracefully. Other fan crazes, such as Star Trek or Harry Potter, undoubtedly inspired similar transitions, but because the Twilight fanpire is almost entirely female, and because the books feature a love story written from a girl's perspective and her explicit views on sex, love, romance, and relationships, it appears calibrated exactly for bonding among women in families. Susan and Gwen would recognize the intention or emotion of the "Twilight Oath," posted online on numerous sites by a fan. It reads in part

Yes, I promise to love Twilight
Wherever I may go
So that all may see my obsession
Because I know what the Twilighters know

The fanpire flourishes in these moments, whether members are alone or part of a giant convention: the shared anticipation for a new film, the glee from purchasing yet another wacky Twilight product, the conviviality of fellow travelers in Forks, and the unbounded joy of mutual recognition. The ephemeral but deeply felt sensibility of "you understand my obsession, and we're in this together" drifts through the fanpire. It's a thoroughly quixotic ideal of belonging and longing for enchantment, the idea that a book and franchise might actually bring you closer to your daughter and to a broader community, allow you to momentarily transcend your ordinary life, transform and fulfill yourself.

After a missed ferry and some circuitous navigation, Susan and Gwen arrive in time for Bella's engagement party at Alice's Closet, a locally owned boutique selling Twilight goods. The festivities throughout the town will include a costume contest, vendors hawking Twilight wares, a Bella birthday celebration, and Quileute storytelling over several days. Despite the hoopla, Forks, an unassuming, spread-out town, is quiet. Except for a banner over one store announcing Stephenie Meyer Day, you might not even notice this was the town's biggest annual event if you were driving through it to the coast.

By 5 p.m., girls and women are milling around the front door of the festively decorated store. A Jasper impersonator hired for the weekend mingles, and a replica of Bella's cake sits on a glass table amidst jewelry, hand-knit items, and signed photographs of cast members. "Bella," bedecked in a tasteful ivory dress and heels, arrives late with "Edward" on her heels. Susan interviews the couple for her Twibond website, asking, "Edward, are you excited to finally get that ring on her finger and seal the deal?" He answers in a somewhat stilted manner, "Yes, I've wanted this since I first met her."

Susan admits that the whirl of activity is the closest she's come to a red-carpet event. She describes herself as "wasted on Twilight," as if visiting Forks is a form of drunken ecstasy.

The faux Bella slices the cake and opens her gifts, demurely flashing her engagement ring to the gathered fans. Gwen and Susan are like jittery brides-to-be. They imagine themselves as girls in the swirl of wedding preparations and expectations, perched on the precipice of something new and slightly terrifying. For Susan, divorced, with two teenagers, and committed to an insurance job in a rural town, Twilight is a portal into a sublime world of conventions, travel, and interviews with Edward. She is a frustrated online dater who demands that potential love interests share her Twilight obsession. One of her dates dozed as they were watching *Twilight*, an unforgivable transgression, and she vowed never to go out with him again. Gwen was just outraged that someone could sleep through the film. For consolation, Susan bought herself a copy of Bella's engagement ring and a facsimile of Bella's floral bedspread.

The Family That Stays Together Preys Together

Throughout the Stephenie Meyer Day weekend, I keep bumping into two women who call themselves "repeat offenders" because they've been back to Forks for Twilight festivities every year since they started, in 2005. They strut into the office of Mike Gurling, the upbeat manager of the Forks visitor center, whose expressive face betrays his devotion to amateur theater, and comment, "Mike, you've lost weight." Erica, who looks eerily like Donatella Versace (and actually held a vigil outside Gianni Versace's home when he was killed), wore rimless, reflective sunglasses pushed up on her blinding white hair. She met Noemi, wide-eyed and whippet thin, at a Stephenie Meyer Day celebration years ago and have continued to be the best of friends. An aspiring paranormal fiction writer, Noemi often dresses as Bella when she visits Forks, and her picture hangs among those of other fans on Mike's office wall. Today with her hennaed hair, slicked straight bangs, and pale skin, Noemi is channeling Hayley Williams, the lead singer of the band Paramore, who contributed several songs to the *Twilight* film soundtrack.

Like Bella, Noemi moved to Washington State from the Southwest without knowing a soul. Unlike Bella, Noemi immediately e-mailed *Twilighters Anonymous*, a popular fan site, and from that day forward had an ever-widening friendship circle of fellow fans. Erica moved to Forks for her husband, and after her marriage fell apart, she found herself unmoored and friendless. Encountering Noemi and others in Forks "helped her through things." She is surrounded by a gaggle of Twilight friends this weekend, pointing out other repeat offenders as we amble through town. Their friendships are predicated on having this place to return to over and over again.

The repeat offenders are a bit like the Cullens in the Twilight saga, a family bound together by common values and beliefs, choice and circumstance rather than by biology. The Cullens are self-defined vegetarian vampires who vow not to harm or kill humans and instead subsist on the blood of animals. Carlisle and Esme Cullen are the stunningly attractive parents of five adopted children, Edward, Alice, Rosalie, Emmett, and Jasper, four of whom are romantically involved with their siblings, yet they still describe themselves first and foremost as a family. Aside from their abstention from human blood, they are a rarity in the world of vampires because they value their kinship over self-preservation. Kinship is a recurrent theme in all the books, with Bella longing to become part of Edward's family and agonizing about leaving her own when she becomes a vampire. Nevertheless, she willingly renounces a mortal life with her own family and friends for vampire immortality with the Cullens, whom she considers a real family and with whom she finally belongs.

A common Twilight fan slogan is "The Family That Preys Together, Stays Together," in reference to the Cullens as the embodiment of an ideal family. Fans also coined the term *Cullenescence*, meaning the essence of all things Cullen. In *The Gospel of Twilight*, a theological assessment of the series, Elaine Heath argues, "Whether one reads Twilight through Protestant, Catholic, Orthodox, or LDS lenses, it is clear that the Cullens are meant to be seen as the exemplary Good Family."[1] She continues, "We have much to learn from the Cullens: two parents that love each other and their children, children with respect for parents, priorities like playing together and protecting each other."[2] They transcend their condition to build "an intentional community of love" and demonstrate compassion, inclusion, and peaceful coexistence with humans and other predatory vampires. They're also filthy rich.

This notion of a family only fits a supernatural coven of vampires because the idea itself is almost supernatural. Most of us would be hard-pressed to name anyone who comes from anything remotely resembling this paradisiacal configuration. My brother once sent me a postcard of a lone man sitting in a giant, empty auditorium where a banner hung reading, "Adult Children of Normal Parents Annual Convention." Despite their enviable bonds, the female Cullens especially are borderline caricatures: Esme, the gentle, maternal figure who restores houses; Alice, party-planner and fashionista; and Rosalie, a sometimes petulant supermodel who just wants a baby. However, in contrast to the Cullens, Bella Swan's parents, Renee and Charlie, are abject failures: immature, inept, and emotionally stunted. Renee is portrayed as an unruly adolescent in her relationship with Bella, and Charlie can't boil a pot of pasta to save his life. It's remarkable he didn't starve to death before Bella moved in with him.

The Quileute wolf pack members, bonded by their transformations into wolves and in their connections to their larger tribe, also exemplify an idyllic community in many ways. However, in contrast to the Cullens, who are prosperous, blindingly white, always impeccably dressed, and representative of the upper class, the Quileutes are depicted wearing torn and casual clothes, and many of their family structures are dysfunctional. Sam, the leader of the wolf pack, has a deadbeat dad, and Embry is a product of his mother's affair with a married man. The books reinforce egregious racial, class, and economic stereotypes that being poor, uneducated, and having dysfunctional relationships are synonymous with the Quileutes, rather than as shortcomings that all families share.[3]

Many critics of the Twilight saga attribute the heavy emphasis on family in the books to Stephenie Meyer's life-long membership in the Mormon Church. Maxine Hanks, a Mormon feminist theologian who was excommunicated from the Church in 1992, lectures widely on Twilight and maintains an avid devotion to Meyer. She is absolutely certain, she says, that Meyer has been shaped by "a Mormon psyche" and compares Meyer to Joseph Smith, because they are visionaries who could see what others could not see.[4] Meyer has stated that the Book of Mormon is the most important text in her life, and many articles have argued that Mormon theology is interwoven into the Twilight texts, especially the ideas of eternal families and celestial marriage.[5]

In the Mormon or LDS Church, families and couples are bound together in sealing ceremonies for eternity. The Mormon ideal of celestial marriage means that you mate for life and beyond in the same way as the vampire Cullens.[6] In the LDS Church, marriage is ordained by God, and once a priest joins a couple in a sealing ceremony in a temple, the marriage bonds extend beyond the husband and wife's earthly lives into the celestial realm.[7] It is a heavenly or divine marriage in which the couple is joined for eternity, as long as they are faithful to the Church's teachings. Only those who are married achieve the fullest possible salvation. The children who are born after the husband and wife make this covenant also automatically partake of their promise, or the children can be sealed to their parents in a special ceremony. The idea is that the entire family endures throughout this life and into the hereafter for all time. This is why members of the LDS Church can retroactively baptize deceased family members in the temple font, extending to them the vicarious possibility of heavenly affirmation.[8]

The Cullens are an ideal LDS family, not least for the fact that they marry forever and exude loyalty and fidelity. One Mormon Twilight fan in Utah told me, "As a member of the Church you understand eternity. But for the world, seeing it from a vampire's point of view really helps [non-Mormons] understand what eternity is in a very material way. You know all those quotes, 'Only a vampire can love you forever'? Well, you know, I know my husband loves me forever, just like a vampire. He always says that, 'I love you like a vampire.'"

The vampires and werewolves in Twilight are devoted monogamists who never fall out of love. In the case of the wolves, imprinting on a mate also joins them for life. Susan says, "I like the idea of the celestial marriage, that love will actually last past the time that you die, and you'll be in the same places and so will your children. I just like that a lot." A Mormon writer noted that the Cullens are less like a coven of vampires and more like the institutional structure of the Mormon Church. "Look at it this way: Carlisle would make an excellent bishop, and Esme, a perfect Relief Society president. Rosalie was born to run a Primary. Emmett would be great leading the Young Men's athletic program. Alice is perfect as ward activities director. Edward could be the Sunday School president. Jasper would hike the Explorer troop's feet to the knees, and with all that cooking and housekeeping experience, Bella would excel as Relief Society homemaking teacher."[9]

Despite the numerous scholarly analyses of the Twilight books as a Mormon text, many LDS members don't actually agree that parallels exist. Deseret Book, the official publisher and global distributor of LDS texts, initially carried the Twilight series, but pulled it from their bookstores. The Twilight saga is now available by special order only. When I visited their main store in Salt Lake City, there was no evidence of Twilight anywhere, a stark contrast to the tables of merchandise and books at nonreligious stores like Barnes and Noble. One of the men working at the Deseret store whispered to me that patrons had complained about Twilight's content, and I have frequently heard and read LDS fans decrying the fact that Edward spends the night in Bella's bed as inappropriate and even risqué. Gail Halladay, the Deseret director of communications and marketing, wrote to me that the company doesn't "consider it to be prudent business practice to take valuable shelf space for such titles." "Some of our customers love the Twilight series while others feel that it addresses content too mature for a teen reader audience," she added.

For Erica, Noemi, Susan, and Gwen, however, the Cullens are appealing as a familial model because, in fact, they are far from the flawless nuclear family enshrined in LDS theology. By the conclusion of the Twilight series, their extended kinship network consists of humans, vampires, half-human/half-vampire babies, and wolf- and vampire-human pairings. Even if their alternative family based on shared convictions might serve as an emblem for multigenerational households, queer kinship, coparenting, and childless and non-monogamous relationships, the Cullens are still all heterosexually married and paired off. In the Twilight saga, those who aren't in a heterosexual couple either die or are condemned to unhappiness, like Leah Clearwater, the sole female member of the wolf pack. Within the limitations of the books' vision, divorced, single, childless fans defy the Mormon underpinnings of the series to emulate the flawed but idealistic bond of the Cullens, even if they can't approximate their physical superiority and outsize wealth.

Glittering Idols

While admirable or even enviable for some, are the Cullens worthy of worship? Imagine someone who treats *Twilight* as a holy book, interprets its passages, emulates the behavior of the Cullens, and makes a pilgrimage to Forks. This could just be a run-of-the-mill Twilight fan. But there's also a group of people who have riled up fans and detractors alike by declaring themselves devotees of something resembling a religion called Cullenism.[10] As one member explained in a forum on *Twifans*, where you log in for church on Sunday, "Cullenism is a mass group of people, referred to as Cullenites, who have come together to appreciate the values and ideals represented by the Twilight series. We are not a religion (or a cult, lol). But we will be comparing and discussing Twilight with religion. We are non-denominational and don't intend to make anyone give up their own personal beliefs to be a part of the Cullenism group. We are simply fans who cherish the values of Twilight (not just how cute Edward is)!" Another says that there "is not a limit to what you can believe in when it comes to the Cullenism religion. . . . We will accept any other Cullenism beliefs you may have." Some fan-site owners, like Amanda Bell of *Twilight Examiner*, drew the line between healthy obsession and religious blasphemy. "I love *Twilight* just as much as the next person, but is it possible for the devotion to have gotten out of hand on this one? I think being obsessed with the books and movies and the actors/characters is one thing. But having it as a religion is taking it too far."[11]

The distinction between the supposed sacrilege of Cullenism and the myriad pleasures of fandom is blurry. What's wrong with designating as religious fan practices such as carefully reading and parsing the books for wider messages, having a sense of belonging to something greater than yourself, or making it a weekly ritual to log on to a website?[12] To oppose Cullenism as an imposter religion presupposes that we know religion when we see it, and that it is always distinct from popular culture, when in fact, the two are invariably commingled and multivalent. Some scholars have argued that as membership in mainline religious denominations declines, elements of popular culture have become sacralized and infused with religious meaning.[13]

There has been a great deal of both scholarly and mainstream hand-wringing over "religious nones," a category that designates the 25 to 30 percent of American adults who purport to have no religious affiliation, a fourfold increase from previous generations.[14] These "nones" aren't necessarily atheists and may have traditional ideas about God, but they tend to feel disaffected with organized religion. One minister complained in the *Washington Post* that these "spiritual but not religious" nones are rootless, dull, self-obsessed, and vapid.[15] They confine themselves to having "deep thoughts all by oneself" rather than doing what the minister called the arduous work of community building within existing religious institutions. They may be more likely to seek the sacred in something like Twilight.

The contention that a spiritual community is the provenance of organized religion misunderstands how something like Twilight works. For fans, it is "a sacred text with multiple interpretations and a host of meaningful, fulfilling practices connected with it, and an audience that considers it a timeless and vital source of inspiration."[16] Whether we cordon that off and call it religious is less interesting than the impetus and sentiment behind it, the collective effervescence and even transcendence of being part of the fandom publicly or privately. One Cullenist defended herself on the fan site by comparing Cullenism to worshipping football or fan fiction: "Let's face it, when many of us reread the books, go onto sites such as [reading] fan fiction, it's kinda like you're worshipping the book." Could the *Twi-*

Fans Cullenism site become the seed of a new religious movement? Stranger things had happened.

In the Cullenism online forum, one irate post blasted the "religion" in all-caps, "This would officially make the Twilight fandom a cult." There are those who agree that Cullenism is merely an explicit manifestation of the false idolatry of Twilight in its most pernicious forms. In particular, Christians have weighed in on the series, deeming it everything from gospel, satanic lure, and Christian blueprint to Mormonism disguised. The "Hogwarts Professor," otherwise known as John Granger, claims that the Twilight series is really all about a particular Christian story. I saw the bow-tie-wearing minister, whose books on Harry Potter serve to justify them as Christian to Christians, lecture to a reverent crowd of fans taking copious notes at the Forks Summer School. After disparaging feminists and secular humanists, Granger informed us that in order to understand Twilight we must start with the fundamentals: Edward is God, transcendent. Therefore, all choices made in the books are in relation to God, and *Twilight* is a retelling of the story of Adam and Eve. The apple on the cover of the book is proof enough, he says.[17] As Eve, Bella offers to God (Edward) her self, her life, and her love. She also carries God's baby in a second annunciation. Granger argues, "Those books and films which deliver beneath the horizon the most religious and archetypal imagery and substance will consequently be the most popular. They meet the spiritual hunger most profoundly."

For other readers, love stories like Bella and Edward's, "remind us of the perfect love that God has for us. God intends for romantic love to reflect his deep desire for an intimate relationship with each of us."[18] Another Christian writer admonishes that Twilight dangerously advertises all-consuming romance when nothing should be all-consuming except one's love for God.[19] Dreams of love, sex, and romance via Twilight are not healthy, according to Beth Felker Jones, a professor at Wheaton College, because they encourage us to expend our desire on things other than God, like Edward cutout dolls and tickets to conventions. "We can let go of our glittering Edwards and our other glittering idols and find freedom in Christ to passionately love this life as it's meant to be loved—for the glory and love of God."[20] For still others, Edward is simply a raging virginal sociopath with control issues.[21]

Whether endorsing or condemning, these writers and the numerous books on Twilight's theological matter imply that Twilight has something of religious import to relay to readers. Many churches and clergy members have embraced the series as a way to engage youth groups around issues of sexuality and relationships. At a nondenominational Bible church in Washington State, a woman led a Twilight study group for adults and teenagers, searching for "biblical intent" in the text. The attendees were all women and girls, many of whom clearly relished a religion-sanctioned opportunity to discuss the books each week. Evelyn, the group leader when I attended, wore the prevalent casual church uniform of jeans and a blue cardigan, her face unlined despite the fact that she was approaching forty. When she occasionally laughed or made a point, she swept back her exceptionally long red hair with her hand. She knew the Twilight saga inside and out and could quickly pinpoint the origin of quotes and characters that eluded me. Her two oldest daughters are also fans, she said, and she had decided to "use Twilight for God," to justify and make sense of their Twilight fixation. Evelyn soberly paraphrased Beth Felker Jones, reminding us that there is a slippery slope from a healthy indulgence in our romantic fantasies to having Twilight replace God altogether. We should fantasize about eternity with the presence of God rather than Edward. "Can't we fantasize about both?" asks a twentysomething woman to laughter.

Steve Wolhberg, a conservative Christian writer, is harsher than Evelyn. According to Wohlberg, Edward is a false messiah who entices girls and women to the devil and promises them the wrong kind of blood.[22] Wohlberg has written screeds condemning Harry Potter as witchcraft and exhorting readers that the Edward who appeared to Stephenie Meyer in her dreams "was a demon with a secret, diabolical agenda." Twilight is a "hellish plot" to keep us focused on the wrong kind of blood, that of vampires, instead of that of Christ. "His love is better than that of vampires, including Edward's," writes Wohlberg. "His blood alone can save our souls. In these last days be-

fore He returns, don't let Lucifer divert your heart *to the wrong blood.*"
For those who say Twilight is a pop monstrosity that is destroying
our culture, they need only look to Wolhberg for ammunition.[23]

Twilight's Mecca

Paul Elie writes that a pilgrimage is "a journey undertaken in the
light of a story. A great event has happened; the pilgrim hears
the reports and goes in search of the evidence, aspiring to be an eye
witness."[24] The story that beckons visitors to Forks is that of Twilight.
The pilgrims come from all over, returning again and again to re-
experience the idea that this is the place where they can "travel into
your imagination in real life," as one woman who organized a trip
for 250 members of TwilightMoms describes Forks. Unlike Hogwarts in the Harry Potter stories or the Shire of *The Lord of the Rings*,
the Forks of the Twilight saga is an ordinary town where fans can
visit the high school where Bella and Edward met, perch on Bella's
weathered red truck, and straddle the treaty line between Forks—
vampire territory—and the nearby Quileute reservation, "home" of
the wolf pack where a sign reads, "No Vampires Beyond this Point."
It's immaterial that the truck, classroom, and treaty line were assembled by the town of Forks and the Quileute tribe to satisfy the
legions of Twilight tourists. The fans are thrilled to inhabit the places
of these beloved fictional characters. According to the Forks visitor
center, in July 2010 alone, approximately 19,000 fans trekked to Forks
like supplicants to a holy site, more than the total number of visitors
to the town in all of 2008.

With the entire weekend to twibond, Gwen and Susan decided
that the ideal way to behold the holy spaces of Twilight was through
a Twilight tour. Fifteen of us glided along in a shiny black van with
"Be Safe" carefully stenciled on the back in the cursive script that
Edward writes in. Crowded into the seats were two Mormon mothers and their fifteen-year old daughters, a father-daughter duo from
Spokane, and a harried dad supervising a group of three junior-high
girls. With the economy in a moribund state, a minivacation to Forks
appeals to cash-strapped parents and restless teens. They've each paid
$39 for the Twilight tour, though anyone could find the sights via the

free map courtesy of the Forks visitor center. But then one wouldn't have Curtis, the burly tour guide who leans into the microphone and asks in a deep voice, "Do you twinkle? Do we have any Jacob fans on board?" There are a few enthusiastic shouts from the group of high school girls, and Curtis cranks up Inner Circle's song with the lyrics, "Bad boys, bad boys, what you gonna do? What you gonna do when they come for you?" On the back of Curtis's seat, in that same loopy "Edward" handwriting is a letter that reads, "*Twilight* Fans, although tips are not required, if my friend Curtis gives a good tour, they are greatly appreciated. Edward Cullen." Susan begins filming our journey as soon as the van lurches forward.

The twibonders and their fellow pilgrims parry Curtis's trivia questions with ease. "What kind of math did Bella take in her final semester?" "Calculus." First stop, the Forks welcome sign, a rustic, green billboard that was relocated from its hillside perch after too many fans stumbled down the slope trying to pose with it. Then, the police station where Charlie Swan works (he's out on patrol today), the hospital with Dr. Cullen's parking space, and the high school. At each stop, there is chatter about whether the Bella Burger is just hype, or where to buy a particular Twilight charm bracelet, or where was Edward last sighted. Forks serves as a prism for fans' collective fantasy, allowing them to live momentarily in the marvelous world of the books, and that's what we're doing as the van takes us around town. Other fans call this phenomenon Twilight Syndrome, a condition characterized by symptoms like a lost sense of reality, hallucinations of Edward Cullen, and the belief that vampires are real.

Normally, fans must content themselves to peer awkwardly through the windows on the wrap-around porch of the Cullen house, a two-story bed and breakfast owned by the Millers, who have gamely entered into the spirit of things by agreeing to remodel their home as the residence of the Cullens. They usually leave notes for visiting fans: "The Cullen family (and Bella) have gone to Fairbanks to check out the University of Alaska." Today we're in luck. As we're jostling for pictures, the door opens and they beckon us inside. The Millers have just acquired a seven-foot case stacked with rows of high school graduation caps in dusky purple, blue, and maroon hues, donated by fans, like the one that hangs in the Cullen home in the film *Twilight*. The Cullen siblings are trapped in eternally youthful bodies and thus condemned to repeat high school over and over as the family moves from town to town to avoid suspicion. Although how a group of luminous-skinned supermodels with orange eyes pass as normal at a typical American high school eludes me. As Edward deadpans to Bella in the first film, "We've graduated a lot."

As we watch, a handyman is affixing the graduation-cap piece onto a wall. While the cameras snap, Gwen glances at a battered upright piano covered with framed photos of Edward and his vampire brothers and sisters. "This isn't Edward's piano," she comments. "Edward plays a black, shiny baby grand." The Millers smile indulgently. The artifice becomes flimsy at such times; the glossy film images, the fans' carefully nurtured vision culled from the books, and Forks itself collide awkwardly.[25]

After the initial elation by Forks residents that the series would be filmed on location, Summit Entertainment ultimately deemed Forks too far from metropolitan centers and considered various sites in Oregon and Canada instead. Boosters of Forks, such as Curtis, emphasize that their town embodies the authentic Twilight, not the glossy film version of it. But even the lack of verisimilitude is not enough to dissuade Gwen and Susan from shooting dozens of photographs and exclaiming giddily over Edward's photograph on the piano lid. Gwen used to keep an Edward life-size cutout in her room, but she soon disposed of it. "Have you ever had a life-size cutout in your room? It's creepy, especially at night." We hear rumors that a woman tracked down the original Volvo Edward owns in the film, purchased it, and has driven it to Forks today. Sure enough, there is a silver Volvo parked by the Forks Motel. It's proof that you can own a piece of your fantasy world.

↝

There are those for whom the siren call of Forks is so powerful that they become permanent residents. Then, professional and everyday lives merge seamlessly with the Twilight fantasy. Curtis's wife, Adrianna, convinced him to move to Forks from Las Vegas because of her fixation with Twilight. He worked as a correctional officer at the maximum-security prison at Clallam Bay, the only major employer in the Forks area outside of the logging industry, until the tour opportunity arose. Originally from Texas, Janine gratefully ditched a parched southwest landscape and now works in marketing and communications at the Forks visitor center. Part of her job is to send out relocation information packets to fans, but she warns them to visit when it's rainy and grim as well. Andrea Mulligan, a retired teacher from North Carolina who founded a Twilight reading group for middle-school students, retired to Forks with her husband and daughter and is now an organizer of Stephenie Meyer Day. Annette Root, a determined woman with a bushy shock of red hair, quit her sixteen-year career as a social worker and moved her entire family to Forks in 2008 from Vancouver, Washington, 250 miles away. She opened the Disney-inspired store Dazzled by Twilight and a performance space that inspired other merchants to start selling Twilight products but was eventually plagued by merchant rivalry (someone described her tenure in Forks as "When Dazzled Attacked"), and financial mismanagement, forcing it to close. All of these people came to Forks to create a Twilight life in the town where their beloved books take place. As one fan slogan sums it up, "I never got my letter to Hogwarts, so I'm moving to Forks to live with the Cullens."

A Place to Shine

There is the desire to live in Forks but also the one to escape. Twilight is a text about transformation through love, a gruesome birth, and a horror-film transfiguration into a vampire. What Bella represents beyond awkward girlhood is every young woman's secret wish to turn into something extraordinary. In *Breaking Dawn*, Bella describes this process after she has become a vampire:

> After eighteen years of mediocrity, I was pretty used to being average. I realized now that I'd long ago given up any aspirations of shining at anything. I just did the best with what I had, never quite fitting into my world. So this was really different. I was amazing now—to them and to myself. It was like

I had been born to be a vampire. The idea made me want to laugh, but it also made me want to sing. I had found my true place in the world, the place I fit, the place I shined.

How many of us can say this about our lives? As Jana Riess has written, Bella shows us the promise of a resurrected, perfect body.[26] We may not become vampires, but why not strive for that place in the world where we stand out? Gwen has already begun the process of metamorphosis. She's left her public high school and enrolled in an online school where she'll complete her junior and senior years. She doesn't have to contend with the travails of high school, mean girls, or even sitting in a classroom. She can complete her homework on the flight across country and spend two weeks in Los Angeles for the premiere of *Breaking Dawn–Part 1* without missing school. Susan, too, disgruntled by her job, even if as Gwen boasts proudly of her mom, "she's really good at it," has reinvented herself as the organizer for a group of Twilight moms, a blogger, and a fan extraordinaire.

The Twilight saga proffers the hope that you, too, may encounter your better self, someone else shinier and more extraordinary. If it happens in a sweltering parking lot behind Leppell's flower shop, aka Twilight headquarters in Forks, so be it. Here, fifty or so fans are gathered expectantly for the annual Stephenie Meyer Day costume contest. Despite Forks's reputation for dreary weather, it's the hottest weekend of the year, so we're wedged against a crumbling but cool brick wall to escape the sun's merciless glare. The contestants begin to assemble on a shaded loading dock: A ten-year-old girl dressed as Jane with a hooded cloak and implacable face . . . a mini-Edward in a gray polo shirt and sunglasses . . . a post-honeymoon Bella, who sweeps in late swathed in a bed sheet, pillow fluff in her hair, bruises smudged on her arms, and clutching a pillow to her chest . . . Bella in her prom regalia . . . a leggy Rosalie Hale in a tight black cocktail dress . . . a few versions of pixiesh Alice . . . a grisly looking Aro, the ruthless Volturi vampire . . . a shirtless James in jeans and a ponytail with skin that glistens with some kind of glitter.

Some are repeat offenders, and some are trying their luck at winning for the first time. As they strut around the courtyard interacting with onlookers, they remain in character: silent Jane, preening Rosalie, growling James, flighty Alice, and, big shock, stumbling Bella. Even when the contest is over and Jane inexplicably loses, she flashes me a hateful stare when I tell her she was robbed. These people inhabit Twilight for a time, urged on by a crowd of fellow fans who are attuned to every nuance of appearance and personality trait.

The professional impersonators—Edward, Bella, Jasper, Alice, and Rosalie (Emmett is said to be off hunting somewhere since the impersonator for his role couldn't be found)—hired for the weekend, hover in the shade, looking at the contestants with slight disdain. They're simply higher up in the food chain of Twilight celebrity.

Earlier, I'd chatted with "Jasper," who slipped in and out of his feigned genteel Southern accent as his curly marmalade-colored wig wobbled on his head. He assured me he was replacing it tomorrow. His specialty is Johnny Depp characters like Sweeney Todd and Jack Sparrow, but he's happy to oblige fans and channel Jasper, even if doing so is an unwelcome reminder of his ex-girlfriend, who used to play Alice. After the costume contest, I snap a picture with the impersonators, and Edward squeezes my shoulder and asks the requisite question of whether I'm Team Edward or Jacob. The impersonators confess that the gig is merely a jumping-off point for potential acting careers, invitations to Twilight conventions, or the possibility of an audition for a pilot. They have plans that extend beyond Twilight, schemes for celebrity and stardom.

Gwen also has a dream of self-transformation. Part of her virtual schooling means she can pursue acting, acknowledging that college is completely unappealing to her. She and Susan fantasize about picking up and moving from Maryland to California, anywhere in California, as part of their dream of starting afresh. That's the lustrous promise of Twilight, to be born again as someone more amazing. A few months later Gwen and Susan will travel to Los Angeles for the Twilight convention and camp out for days with 900 other fans before the *Breaking Dawn* premiere in order to glimpse the stars on the red carpet. They'll form a living circle with their newfound group, holding hands and rotating as they gradually approach the Summit Entertainment representative who is doling out wristbands that grant permission to enter camp city. They'll feel the elation of just talking, pressing against another's shoulder, hearing their voices echoing with others. After days together in the parking lot, they'll have survived the experience of awaiting the premiere, bonded to legions of others with the same aspirations, embarking upon a kind of public happiness absent from the day to day. As Susan puts it, "That's how we bond."

The bond resides in the mutual agreement by fans, residents, and onlookers to allow the real and fantastical to merge briefly. For Gwen, Susan, and the other van riders on the tour of Forks, it is not a stretch to imagine that the impenetrable curtain of green forest encasing Forks, even on a sunny, resplendent day, conceals vampires and werewolves, and that the droning roar from the drag races at the track is a pitched battle between the wolves and vampires. When Mike Gurling says sadly that the Forks movie theater burned down in the fall, Janine whispers that she knew what happened: Edward's battle with James, a vengeful vampire, ignited the blaze. *Twilight* and other recent vampire books assume the supernatural as a facet of everyday life, and for fans, the boundary between the paranormal and the real world is porous. The fans I spoke to and surveyed almost always have a traditional religious affiliation, but they also profess belief in a supernatural pantheon of vampires, shape-shifters, angels, and aliens.[27]

On our van tour, many are disgruntled by the sun since, they say half-joking, it means glimpsing a vampire will be more difficult (Twilight vampires break with genre and sparkle in the sun rather than risk slow obliteration by it, but they still avoid it. On sunny days, the entire Cullen family is usually absent from school). As Maxine Hanks writes, "For readers, Twilight is a waking dream, a myth that lives." In various high schools near San Antonio, Texas, groups of kids have formed their own wolf packs with alpha leaders and sometimes wear leashes, fangs, and chains.[28] In an article about the phenomenon, one of the participants says he doesn't believe anyone is just human, rather that we're all harboring some other persona deep down and that we just have to look inside and find it. Their packs are a form of family. "You get friends. You get a place where you belong. You're pretty much accepted to where you are, who you are, what you are," said sixteen-year-old Adrian Baine Manl, known as Deikitsen Wolfram Lupus, a member of one of the packs. Tragically, Deikitsen, who found solace and belonging in his pack, had a tempestuous home life, was bullied at school, and, in 2010, hanged himself.[29] He is now remembered on Facebook, MySpace pages, and YouTube videos as a part of the wolf pack. Susan seems to echo the wolf pack's sentiment of transcending the rigidity of social expectations for behavior in her own way: "I ask myself, how can we bear to live in a world that is all fact, in which every answer can be tallied up like a mathematical equation?"

At one end of Forks, just where the road stretches to nowhere, Marcia Bingham, an energetic woman in her early fifties, presides over the Forks Chamber of Commerce with the aid of her furry terrier and an array of employees. She's wearing a "Team Jacob" pin and is gesticulating to tourists next to a giant, cutout picture of Edward Cullen slouching against the main door. In 2006, a trickle of sheepish fans arrived at the center, guilt-ridden and embarrassed, offhandedly mentioning they were in Forks because of the Twilight books. There was none of the camaraderie or commotion around the series then, but Marcia quickly learned to "speak Twilight," and decided to render what she calls the Twilight tourists' "dirty little secret" unnecessary. Mike Gurling says he knew that his town was forever changed when an airport security person spotted his Forks shirt and detained him merely to chat about how much he loved the books.

To keep track of the 500 to 700 *Twilight* tourists that the visitors center says arrive in town per day, volunteers there keep a tally on a three-inch pile of wrinkled yellow notepaper, which they add up at the end of the month. The log bursts with the all-caps enthusiasm of swooning fans: "Thanks for speaking *Twilight!*" and "At last my wife can stop nagging!" Before the deluge, Mike used to take photographs of fans to post on the visitor center website. When he had accumulated 900 pictures, he realized their server couldn't hold any more.

While we're at the visitor center, a group of girls barrel through the door and gleefully shriek, "Ohmygodohmygodohmygod!" as they ricochet from one part of the room to another. Earlier that day the center had hosted a group of self-described Twilight widows, not the men of the tongue-in-cheek blogs that complain they've been abandoned by Twilight-besotted wives but a group of women who have lost their spouses and found each other through the *Twilight-Moms* forum. Twilight is the surrogate for their loss, a therapeutic means of working through their grief and replacing it with a comradeship of equal parts fortification and frivolity.

The high school volunteer answering the phones at the visitor center, the son of the local newspaper editor, informs a caller, "There have been a few vampire sightings," in response to a question about visiting the nearby Quileute Indian reservation. The sense of the supernatural is precisely what captivates the fans who arrive in droves, and Marcia, the visitor center director, and the others gallantly acquiesce. Marcia offhandedly remarks, "I live in a fantasy world here," as if it's a joke they're all in on, relishing the giddiness of inhabiting the world of Twilight even while the grittier reality of Forks encroaches. One woman writes that day in the visitor center log book, "Just a couple of girls looking for a couple of vampires or wolf boys." Susan explains, "I do understand the difference between fact and fiction, but we all need a little magic and fantasy in our life. . . . We wanna pretend together. And we do, and I don't think there's anything wrong with that. I still do the dishes; I still scrub the toilet, just like everybody else."

The final tour stop is the town of La Push on the Quileute reservation. Fans can also visit later that night to hear Chris Morganroth, a storyteller and member of the Quileute tribe, recount traditional legends around a bonfire at First Beach. In the Twilight books, Stephenie Meyer identifies Jacob Black's house as a sprawling red bungalow where he repairs motorcycles. The tour van pulls up next to one of similar description with the fortuitous coincidence of being owned by a person with the surname Black. Jacob's father in the books is named Billy and here "B. Black" is stamped on the mailbox. Between the mailbox, motorcycle, and pictures of Jacob in the window, the illusion is complete.

The fans and the franchise unabashedly romanticize the Native American tribes of the Pacific Northwest. One white, middle-age woman was bedecked in what she called Native jewelry and was raving about meeting actual Native Americans. In the movies *New Moon* and *Eclipse*, the members of the wolf pack are continually shown bare-chested, all the better to gawk at their shiny muscles. The books endlessly describe their muscularity and ravenous eating habits. The seclusion of the reservation and the invisibility of Native Americans in general outside of their fantastical portrayal in the books, along with fans' cursory knowledge of American Indian history, imbue La Push with an enchantment that is sometimes tinged with racism and sentimentality. Despite an attempt by the tribe to counter and debunk some of these perceptions, and a recent exhibition at the Seattle Art Museum entitled *The Real Quileutes*, the Native characters and actual people often stand in for the supernatural and mystical for fans. Some of this stereotype is mitigated by the fact that conditions in La Push are far from glamorous, and the residents look like people everywhere else, contrary to some fan assumptions.

The tour stops. On a promontory at First Beach, an arrestingly desolate stretch of coast strewn with driftwood, we glimpse the barren James islands, the rocky tips of the sea stacks considered sacred to the Quileute tribe. In the distance are the sheer cliffs where Bella recklessly plunges into the churning water in *New Moon*. Susan eagerly cranes her head out the van's window as we approach and appears dazed by the scenery. For the first time that day, we're outdoors for an extended period, without a house, restaurant, store, police station, truck, or visitor center to distract us. However, the lack of Twilight infrastructure is a stark reminder that the Quileute tribe has fewer economic resources than Forks, and there are complaints that Forks profits at the expense of the reservation. The coffee kiosk with the title "Jacob's Java" is no doubt a harbinger of imminent Twilight tourism, especially given that the tribe has hired a public relations specialist to cope with the barrage of requests for interviews and visits.

Like all pilgrims, we must eventually return home from our journey, and the magic of our trip is broken as we disembark from the van and head off separately. The pilgrimage is not quite over yet, however, because Susan is dead set on finding the meadow where Bella and Edward fall in love, agree to marry, and kiss. Susan, her daughter Gwen, and I set out with vague, probably concocted directions from a volunteer at the visitor center, following a footpath leading from the drag-racing track across the street. The trail is indecipherable and spooky. We double back twice, consult our map, and consider abandoning the endeavor altogether, but I find a mixture of pleasure and absurdity in our nonsensical quest. It's not too late to stumble upon some enchanted place. And then, serendipitously, a lush expanse with a few late-blooming foxgloves and wildflowers opens before us. This is a meadow worthy of *Twilight*, and for a brief moment, it's possible, if we squint hard enough, to glimpse a girl and a vampire lying entwined in the sun.

Eclipse

Bella has a dilemma that afflicts girls and women everywhere: two gorgeous supernatural men are devoted to her and fight each other to prove who loves her most. Bella wavers between Edward and Jacob throughout the book, and all three even pass an awkward night together in a tent, but there is no sex. Jacob, whose normal body temperature runs around 108.9 degrees snuggles next to Bella in the sleeping bag while Edward, all ice-cold muscles, huddles beside them and seethes with jealousy as he reads Jacob's lascivious thoughts. "I am Switzerland. I refuse to be affected by territorial disputes between mythical creatures," Bella declares to both rivals. Why are they in a tent together on a mountain in a blistering snowstorm? Because a newborn vampire army is preparing to lay siege to the unsuspecting town of Forks, so Bella, Jacob, and Edward hide while the Cullens and the Quileute wolves join forces to battle the army.

Aside from the love triangle, *Eclipse* is about the power of the Cullens' bond and the temporary allegiance of the wolf pack and the vampires. We learn more about the Cullen family in flashbacks and what makes them the ultimate loyal, nonbiological family. Carlisle lived for a time with the Volturi and turned Edward into a vampire when Edward was dying of the Spanish influenza. Rosalie was gang raped and left for dead by her fiancée until Carlisle saved her. She later avenges the crimes and murders each rapist one by one. Emmett was gored by a bear, Alice was confined to a mental asylum, and Jasper was a major in the Civil War. Meanwhile, Bella decides that Edward is the only one she truly loves, and they continue to declare their undying love for each other. "The outside world holds no interest for me without you," Edward tells her. At the end of the book, once the vicious vampire army and Bella's nemesis are defeated, Bella decides that yes, she will marry Edward, but he must promise to have sex with her as a human first.

CHAPTER 4

The Forbidden Fruit
Tastes the Sweetest

Edward Cullen is a twentysomething ruthless CEO who meets Bella when she interviews him for her college newspaper. They experience a magnetic attraction, but he harbors a nasty secret: the only way he can have a relationship with Bella is if she agrees to sign a written contract agreeing to be his submissive in a bondage relationship. At one point, when Bella asks, "Does this mean you're going to make love to me tonight, Edward?" his response is, "No Isabella, it doesn't. Firstly, I don't make love. I fuck . . . hard. Secondly, there's a lot more paperwork to do. And thirdly, you don't yet know what you're in for and you could still run for the hills. Come. I want to show you my playroom."

Is this the Twilight series you've come to know and love? No, it is "Master of the Universe," once one of the most popular stories on Twilighted.net, a massive Twilight fan-fiction site. (In its new incarnation as *Fifty Shades of Grey*, it's the number-one book on Amazon .com.) Just one of the thousands of reviews of "MofU" raves: "I've mentioned in my reviews that MofU is my own special brand of heroin, an addiction I will have to go into rehab for." "MofU" and others aren't short stories but epics, and to read them all would be a full-time job as there are thousands of entries and a constant supply of submissions to the site. As authors post chapters, fans can heckle or encourage. One fan of "MofU" said, "I love this story. It has hijacked my life for nearly two weeks. I just keep reading and re-reading and pondering." In some fan-fic, the Twilight characters are all human (AH); in others, Edward is a computer geek or cocky bartender (Canon or Fanon). A more humorous genre (Crackfic) makes fun of the characters, like a shopaholic Alice who needs addiction therapy.

By far the most prolific stories, and the ten consistently rated as "most read," are what writers informally call "smut," a genre that envisions the relationships in Twilight as sexually explicit. In this lively universe, the authors, primarily women, pen erotic scenes between Bella and Edward and fulfill their desires for salacious sexuality. There is a storyline for every proclivity: slash or femslash with sex scenes between Jasper and Edward, or alternate romantic pairings like Leah Clearwater and Edward. Known to readers by pen names like IceSnowDragon and Twilightzoner, these authors are beseeched for more chapters, chastised for writing OOC (out of character), and cheered for the UST (unresolved sexual tension) or pure smuttiness: "Holy hell another change of panties!!! lol . . . Viola that's not fair, I just had a change like 1 hour ago!!!" Twilightzoner, a renowned smut author with sarcasm in abundance, describes the genre as "missing moments" that usually take place in an AU (alternate universe) that is AH (all human). Authors feel compelled to eliminate the supernatural characters, because to try to adhere to the Twilight canon by inserting explicit sex is an oxymoron.

The most-favored smut stories still feature Edward and Bella. Instead of meadows and innocent kisses, there is promiscuity, sexual abuse, incest, bondage, sex addiction, and, of course, some romance. In "The Training," Bella "lives to serve her Master. It can be tedious at times, titillating at others, but always, her world revolves around his. Come take a peek at the trials and triumphs in the life of a 24/7 consensual slave and find what happens when outside forces threaten to expose her lifestyle." Bella meets Edward when she visits his roommate Jasper and awakens to find him nuzzling her in "Never Sleep in a Strange Man's Bed." During the weeks leading up to her wedding, a sexually frustrated Bella writes "The List," cataloguing all the ways she'd like to have sex with Edward once they're married. "To Do: Against the tree in the meadow, on our lab table, on his leather couch . . ." The tagline reads: "She's surprised to find she might be able to cross some things off earlier than she thought . . ."

Twilightzoner explains the appeal of smut fan-fic this way, "I was tired of grasping at crumbs and the fact that there is no follow-through. As adult women, we miss that. We're like, 'Bella, you're missing out, girl!'" According to Twilightzoner, because the series is young adult, smut is an attempt to fill in the blanks and "elevate the maturity level." One of Twilightzoner's most notorious stories, "Midnight Desire," features Edward fantasizing about Bella's breasts during their first meeting in the biology lab. The story swiftly becomes more graphic. It is a parody of "Midnight Sun," Stephenie Meyer's derailed manuscript that envisions Twilight from Edward's perspective. When someone leaked "Midnight Sun" on the Internet, Meyer cast the story aside out of, she said, a sense of violation. In the smut version, Twilightzoner replaced all the vampirism with sex. "No blood lust—just *extreme* human lust. AH/AU and consequently, OOC," she writes on Twilighted.net. Reading Twilight smut is similar to devouring a risqué romance novel. The stories are silly, heart-racing, and often raunchy. Those who want the missing moments Twilightzoner mentions find the scenes of Edward and Bella having sex against the tree in their favorite meadow deeply satisfying.

Fans might want more sex in their literature, but they also adore the Twilight series and watch the films endlessly perhaps in part because of the delayed gratification, or what critics call the "erotics of abstinence."[1] Readers are forced to wait, too, enduring countless scenes of almost-seduction, temptation, and barely restrained lust so that we're rooting for them to succumb at last and are mesmerized by the sexual postponement. They read and watch voraciously because of Bella and Edward's all-consuming attraction to one another and the necessity of resisting it. Their sexual tension fuels their romantic fever and, by extension, ours. After all, throughout the series, Edward tells Bella he cannot do more than kiss her despite her pleas. His iron will might falter, and he would ravage her sexually and bloodily. They spend hours cuddling, nuzzling, kissing, gazing, and tempting each other in Bella's living room and bedroom, as these lines from *New Moon* indicate, in which Bella says,

"No, I want you to kiss me again."

[EDWARD:] "You're overestimating my self-control."

"Which is tempting you more, my blood or my body?" . . .

"It's a tie."

One critic has dubbed the Twilight series "abstinence porn" to describe the characters' suppressed desire for one another.[2] The clamor by many writers about Twilight as solely an abstinence-only tract, though, misses why girls and women relish the books. PsyMom, a statuesque woman in her early forties and a well-known BETA, that is, someone who reviews fan-fic stories before they go live on Twilighted.net sums up this sentiment. "No sex is the new sex," she says at the fan-fic workshop. "When [characters] kiss, we've been so deprived that it's like, 'wheeeee.'"

These moments of postponement and abstinence are ubiquitous: the numerous tentative attempts to kiss in *Twilight*, the lingering moments where Bella clings to Edward, grabbing fistfuls of his blue shirt after her failed birthday in *New Moon*, their impassioned kisses in the meadow at the beginning of *Eclipse*. The tension is infuriating and seductive. "The relationship between Bella and Edward is sweet and old-fashioned," one woman remarked on the Twilighted .net forum, "yet the sexual tension between them is a big turn-on."

The erotic tension and the sense of being poised on a sexual precipice disappear in smut. Bella and Edward have sex within the first few chapters of most fan-fic stories, so fans gain sexual explicitness but lose what is arguably the most powerful, reviled, and delectable aspect of the series. In *Breaking Dawn*, before they have sex, the smallest gestures bespeak oceans of longing and desire: fingers brushing against one another briefly, scorching glances, and a kiss as the culminating erotic moment. It's no coincidence that Stephenie Meyer is a fan of British women writers like Jane Austen or that she has Bella reading *Wuthering Heights* in the books, however farfetched the idea is of Catherine Earnshaw or Elizabeth Bennett asking, "So what you're saying is, I'm your brand of heroin?"

Fans' longings for the abstinence porn of the Twilight narrative *and* the smut of fan-fic suggests that the way sexuality is experienced by many girls and women is schizophrenic and contradictory. The books champion abstinence in explicit ways, but Bella's insistent sexual desire undermines some of the tenets of abstinence-only education. Her lust must be held in check by a stalwart Edward rather than by the typical premise of purity culture that girls rein in the base proclivities of young men. Even if Bella desires sex, though, she's never promiscuous or slutty, a message that does not always reverberate in the hook-up culture prevalent for some teenagers and college-age women. Bella's romance with Edward is predicated on his being a perfect gentleman with a dash of danger thrown in. Ultimately, though Edward professes undying love for her, he also leaves her bruised, battered, and pregnant with a vampire/human hybrid after their first sexual experience on their honeymoon, eerily mimicking markers of domestic violence and rape.

Smut writers and their readers grapple with these incongruous ideas of sexuality in Twilight and the broader culture, cleverly and obsessively reimagining the characters. Fan fiction is a tribute to a story they love and can't let go of, and so they possess, rework, and critique the material by creating a parallel universe and expanding an already existing archive.[3] In *Textual Poachers*, Henry Jenkins suggests that fan fiction allows audiences opportunities to "play with the rough spots of a text—its narrative gaps, its excess details, its loose ends and contradictions—in order to find openings for the fans' elaborations of its world and speculations about characters."[4] Smut fan fiction in particular counters Twilight's insistence on abstinence with explicit, racy sex. They champion female desire but also revert to romance novel conventions about purity and virginity.

There are also sly critiques of the idea that sex leads to unintended pregnancies, too. In "Never Sleep in a Strange Man's Bed," when the fan-fiction author forgot to include condoms in one scene, she immediately replied to readers, "This was unintentional! I got caught up in the moment. Please, assume they are [there] and I'll try to go back and fix those scenes when I can. There will be no surprise pregnancies for them and they have better sense than that. As we all should!" The moral of Twilight and even some of the most prurient fan-fic stories is that sex is accompanied by love and romance as long as the heroine is pure in some way. In "Master of the Universe," Edward expects a reluctant Bella to engage in whippings, handcuffing, and other bondage games. Bella eventually loses her virginity to Edward in what he considers "vanilla sex" and in so doing begins to reform him from damaged, sexual master to loving husband.

Keeping It Real

Although fan-fiction smut writers and readers dwell primarily in the realm of the virtual, I met some of the denizens of this vast world at a workshop entitled "Fade to Black . . . Twilight's Missing Moments" at TwiCon. The nine other fan-fiction workshops focused on topics such as "Jacob Black in Fan-Fiction: From Hindrance to Hero" and "Robward, Kellmett and Jacksper: The Impact of the Movies on Fan-fic." The "smut" workshop promised to explain, according to its description, why the Twilight fan-fiction stories "have become some of the most popular in the fandom." In a generic conference room packed entirely with women who were mainly over thirty and white, writers and readers debated abstinence, realistic sex, and just what constitutes smut.

Four fan-fic smut luminaries—Twilightzoner, PsyMom, OCD (Obsessive Cullen Disorder), and Ninapolitan—fielded questions. Looming over the folding table where the three authors sat was a life-size cutout of Robert Pattinson as Edward: pinup idol, patron saint, and smut inspiration. The women were dressed casually in t-shirts either designating the wearer as a member of the Vampire baseball league or, a fan favorite, bearing the slogan "The Forbidden Fruit Tastes the Sweetest." The women know each other by their pen names and are intimately familiar with the stories the panel discusses. The chummy atmosphere is like a meeting of a secret club where people casually refer to intricate plot details in stories such as "How Do Dirty Boys Get Clean" and "Blue Flower."

Smut may be a counterpoint to the chaste fairy tale of Twilight, but it wasn't usually any more realistic. Should they portray sexuality in all its potential awkwardness for younger readers? Twilightzoner, PsyMom, and OCD wondered aloud. They discussed, for instance, whether to write about their husbands' bumbling attempts to seduce them, ultimately abandoning the idea because, they said, no one would want to read those stories. Jenwordsong, a prolific writer in the audience, calls out, "No one wants to read, 'He rolls over [and says,] Hey, you wanna?' or, 'Turn the TV up,'" to which the room responds with rollicking laughter.

Jenwordsong was concerned that so many young women read their stories despite Twilighted.net's requirement that readers be over seventeen. Younger writers and readers are not supposed to submit stories or reviews on *Twilighted*, but other fan-fiction websites have no such restrictions. And if I wanted a more sexually explicit site with no editing, the woman next to me whispered conspiratorially, I should check out *Twigasm*. It's impossible to enforce someone's age or verify their identity online, and, according to Twilightzoner, young women are also writing "phenomenal" stories and "really good smut." For a time, she had a fourteen-year-old from Norway reading and commenting on "Midnight Desire." Twilightzoner says with a laugh, "They're more liberal in Norway. Besides, my story isn't all smut, just sprinkled with smut."

Unrealistic depictions of first sex as mind-blowing and multi-orgasmic, a convention of romance novels, are pervasive in fan-fic stories. Younger readers, Twilightzoner says, weaned on romance novels expect to have a simultaneous orgasm their first time with a boy. The smut writers agonize about whether their stories do girls a disservice. PsyMom asks the room, "What is our responsibility as writers? Should we make it realistic?" In the fan-fic story "Midnight Desire," Bella has a realistic first time in which the sex is not particularly enjoyable, but Twilightzoner worries that readers "will hang me because it's not a fantasy experience." PsyMom jokes that Bella's first time wasn't exactly stellar, but the second time was better, so "Midnight Desire" combines reality and fantasy. The consensus is that no one wants to read fiction about boring sex or ungainly first, second, or third times.

Pregnant women having sex is also a huge taboo, says Twilightzoner. "It's real life and it's not perfect, which is not why people read the series." An audience member calls out, "If pregnant women didn't have sex, they wouldn't stay married." Of course, with such a multitude of fan-fic stories, there are exceptions. One of the cheekiest blogs, *The Perv Pack's Smut Shack*, features a "Lemon Report" for recommended stories. The number of lemons denotes the level of a story's sexual explicitness. "Naughty Nurse Kimpy" dispenses sex advice on the blog from how to insert an IUD to how often women should masturbate.

The Perv Pack rapturously reviewed a fan-fic lemon called "Parenthetical Love," which chronicles a mix-up at a fertility clinic. Bella plans to have a baby as a single woman using her gay friend Jasper's sperm, but she ends up with Edward's sperm instead. She and Edward meet and eventually fall in love with a lot of pregnancy sex in between. Edward's point of view: "Touching the silk over [the] solid swell of her baby bump had made him feel almost caveman—all biology and nature with very little thought involved. Kissing her hadn't been enough in that moment. He wanted to pick her up and claim her completely, driving any thought of anyone else out of her mind forever. She was his to have and his to protect." The story may be about assisted reproductive technologies, but it also has substantial pregnancy sex.

This is the classic WussPerv narrative. According to *The Perv Pack's Smut Shack*, a WussPerv is someone who is "Tragically canon, Loathes angst (when in massive doses), Loves smut and Needs a Happy-Ever-After." WussPerv stories, usually featuring Bella and Edward in human or vampire/human form, crowd the top-ten lists of Twilighted.net. In these stories, no matter if Edward is a dominant in a bondage relationship, a "smooth-talking motherfucker" who likes to pick up girls in bars for casual sex, or a commitment-averse architect who has never had a long-term relationship, the stories stick to the canon premise: Bella and Edward are soul mates, destined to be together forever. The most favored stories in the WussPerv category are where the pairings remain the same, romance blossoms, and there is "unf," a fan term for "universal noise of fucking." In "Never Sleep in a Strange Man's Bed," Bella fools around with Edward the first night they meet, but they end up first living together and then happily married with fulfilling careers in sunny North Carolina. Here the distinctions between the Twilight canon and smut are not so stark. The readers want their sex, but they want an idyllic ending, too.

WussPerv smut stories operate as variations on a time-tested romance novel formula: virginal or sexually inexperienced female character (one or maybe two prior sexual partners is the norm for contemporary romances) who is also strong and plucky meets conflicted hero; misunderstandings occur, such as an instant dislike or conflict between the characters or a seemingly insurmountable barrier between them; sexual attraction builds; and true love triumphs. Despite the disdain accorded to the genre, the Romance Writers of America report that 64.6 million Americans read at least one romance novel a year and, in 2005, spent over $1.37 billion on romance. And readers ages eighteen to thirty-four are more likely to read romance than any other age group.[5] The popularity of *Fifty Shades of Grey* is indicative of the insatiable demand for these stories.

In most romance stories, to which WussPerv fan fiction and Twilight are indebted, the male character, who is some combination of jaded, disreputable, flawed, or wounded yet generally honorable, seduces the innocent, plucky, shy, headstrong virgin. To his dismay, he discovers that not only has she awakened his sentimental side along with his flammable desire, but that he also must have her, marry her, and be with her forever at all costs.[6] Romance fiction capitalizes on the idea that both men and women need emotional connections to enjoy sex fully. The WussPerv fantasy, too, is that a relationship initially based solely on sex will turn into something romantic. In "Master of the Universe," Bella's virginity ensnares and entrances Edward, the sexually voracious CEO, until he realizes that his feeling for her are emotional and romantic rather than just sexual, and his treatment of her becomes kind, solicitous, and caring.

Abstinence and Supernatural Sex

At our fan-fiction workshop, Twilightzoner voiced a subversive opinion, at least in the world of fans: "The books are about abstinence, and they're not neutral; they're anti-sex. In the fourth book, married sex kills [Bella] and has consequences." That Bella and Edward desist from any form of sex until marriage for fear that it will kill her is easily read as a thinly veiled argument for abstinence. However, most fans balk at the idea that the books are abstinence-only tracts or that abstinence is necessarily a negative aspect of the series. They read the books literally: Edward must tread carefully or risk killing Bella because he is a vampire, not because the books are a Mormon writer's sinister plot to instill abstinence values in millions of readers. Twilightzoner's comment sparks murmurs of dissent. PsyMom says emphatically of Bella, "She gets what she wants: a husband and a baby."

Today's multifaceted purity movement encompasses everything from abstinence programs such as True Love Waits and the Silver Ring Thing to abstinence-only school curricula.[7] All employ a logic that assumes that wasting sex on a relationship that doesn't end in marriage means there will be less romance left over for the marriage itself, that premarital sex can be harmful and lead to sexually transmitted diseases, and, in the case of religious arguments, that sex is a sacrament reserved for marriage. Delaying sex until marriage ensures unparalleled intimacy and sexual bliss with a future spouse.[8]

Edward is often cited as the epitome of abstinence. The capacity to easily hurt and kill Bella is ever-present, but he possesses the self-control to refrain (except in *Breaking Dawn*). A paragon of the religious arguments for abstinence, Edward is a virgin plagued by thoughts of whether he'll go to heaven. Abstinence, he believes, will preserve the remnants of his soul. Edward's concern for Bella's soul as well, a subject of endless conversation between them, is his rationale for sexual abstinence and his initial refusal to turn her into a vampire.

Twilight was published in 2005, the year the Bush administration spent $270 million on abstinence-only sex-education programs. Edward as the heroic protector is mirrored in abstinence-only textbooks like *Choosing the Best*, which presents a story of a princess who cheekily dispenses advice to a knight about how to kill a dragon. The proud knight is ashamed to accept her help, and he marries someone else. The moral is that if you're too sassy and independent, you won't find a husband.[9] The Twilight series echoes an assumption of abstinence education that sex can be deadly before marriage, except in the

Twilight stories, the danger is vampire venom rather than an STD. And the idea of a resplendent hero who cares about your virtue bolsters cultural campaigns like True Love Waits and virginity pledges. However, studies have shown that of adolescents who took virginity pledges, only 12 percent kept their promise, others engaged in oral sex, and they were one-third less likely to use protection when they did eventually have sexual intercourse.[10] Even in the actual Forks high school, though Washington State requires comprehensive sex education, a poster prominently displayed in a girls' bathroom reads, "Kiss a Toad, and He's Still a Toad. Abstinence 'til Marriage."

Like the Twilight franchise, the abstinence movement succeeds because it is what Dagmar Herzog calls a self-help and self-improvement movement that holds out the promise of perfection.[11] Abstinence enthusiasts vow that it translates to a perfect marriage with a perfect man with whom you will have perfectly fantastic and always heterosexual sex. This idea is part of the abstinence movement's campaign to "make chastity sexy."[12] When, for example, Lesley Unruh of the Abstinence Clearing House hands out cherry lollipops with a heart center that reads, "Don't be a sucker! Save sex for marriage," she implies not only that sex outside of marriage is damaging, dangerous, emotionally draining, and shameful but that it's mind-blowing once you're married. Doomsday admonitions about sex and statistics about sexually transmitted diseases fail to convince in the same way as the notion that once married, sex is sensational because you've kept your purity.

This idea dovetails neatly with the premise of much romance fiction, which overvalues virginal heroines who find sexual bliss with their one true love. In countless historical romances, the virgin heroine experiences married sex as emotional and sensual delirium. Twilight's messages about sexuality as dangerous reflect both of these premises of abstinence education and romance fiction: sex is dangerous (you could be sucked dry by your vampire boyfriend) and sex is phenomenal once you're married. It gets even better once you become a supernatural being with preternatural sexual powers.

Twilight emerged in the middle of a boom in paranormal romance and the proliferation of young-adult vampire literature: the number of these books published in the United States doubled between 2002 and 2004. A large proportion of Twilight readers love other paranormal romance stories such as *The Vampire Diaries, True Blood* (based on Charlaine Harris's Southern Vampire Mysteries series), the Anita Blake series by Laurel Hamilton, and *The Dark Hunter* series by Sherrilyn Kenyon. Informally known as "sucking and fucking," the genre features sexual collisions between tough female protagonists and the male horror staple of choice: sexy vampires, kick-ass demon hunters, and testosterone-fueled werewolves. A prominent title in the genre can sell over 500,000 copies.[13] Young-adult paranormals now dominate entire sections at Barnes and Nobles grouped in the genre Teenage Paranormal Romance.[14]

In this category, fantastical vampires, witches, werewolves, and shape-shifters usually coexist with humans without their knowledge. Although some of these novels develop the alternate world with meticulous detail, others focus mainly on the romance between the protagonist (often a human unaware of her powers) and the male supernatural character who awakens her sexually and romantically. One paranormal fan on a blog comments, "With aliens, mermaids, shape-shifters, and the like, we're going into some seriously taboo territory. I mean, what the protagonist is fucking is not even strictly human. Sexy interspecies humping extravaganza, woot. And then there's the whole vampires/familiars/whatever can make the sex sooo much better than normal via vaguely explained mystical means."

While Bella is hardly the supernatural sexual vamp of some of these other paranormal romance books, she does represent its basic trope of a human who is unaware of her powers (Edward can't read Bella's mind like he can everyone else's), and she becomes a fully realized sexual being only after marrying a vampire. The Twilight saga can be read as an abstinence text with a vampire identity substituted for a Christian one: once married and born again as a Christian *or* a vampire, your sex life is unparalleled ecstasy for eternity. It's implied in *Breaking Dawn*, for instance, that vampires experience sexual sensations beyond that of humans. Once Bella becomes a vampire, she describes how sex with Edward is that much more wondrous, and how they never tire so they never have to stop:

He had the most beautiful, perfect body in the world and I had him all to myself, and it didn't feel like I was ever going to find a point where I would think, *Now I've had enough for one day*. I was always going to want more. And the day was never going to end. So, in such a situation, how did we ever *stop*?
It didn't bother me at all that I had no answer.

At our smut workshop, PsyMom asks, "Would the relationship have lasted if they never had sex, and she never became a vampire? Has anyone written about this?" Instead of true love and steamy sex forever, their relationship just fizzles. Twilightzoner quips, "Get a box of Kleenex. That's just sad."

Bad Girls Don't Get Romance

In smut, women are allowed to like sex without being labeled sluts or whores. You don't hear Bella ruminating about her unruly sexual urges in *Twilight* as she does in "Master of the Universe": "My heart beat spikes, and I think I'm panting. Jeez, I'm a quivering, moist, mess and he hasn't even touched me. I squirm in my seat and meet his dark glare. He brings his hand up to grasp my chin and holds me in place. I am helpless, my hands pinned, my face held and his hips restraining me. I can feel his erection against my belly. . . . He wants me. . . . Edward Cullen, Greek god, wants me. And I want him, here now, in the elevator." Even without the explicitness of smut, Twilight upends the abstinence movement's premise that girls control boys' predatory lust while lacking any sexual desire themselves. Twilight Bella implores Edward to have sex. Edward tells her in *Eclipse*, "Do you get the feeling that everything is backward? Traditionally, shouldn't you be arguing my side, and I yours?"

Edward must restrain and vigilantly monitor Bella's increasingly ardent sexual advances rather than the other way around. She is the one who lacks restraint and desperately pleads, cajoles, and even attempts to trick him into sex while Edward firmly and a bit reluctantly rebuffs her. Some typical exasperated comments from Edward include these from *Eclipse*: "Do you have any idea how painful it is, trying to refuse you when you plead with me this way?" or, "Bella.

Would you please stop trying to take your clothes off?" In fan fiction, Bella is often even more sexually forthright. In one smut story by "Lilly Cullen," Bella is so frustrated and fed up by Edward that she goes to Jasper to assuage her needs as a sex-craved newborn vampire. A review on the *Perv Pack Smut Shack* blog reads, "This is a wicked dirty Jasper/Bella smuttake. Bella is an insatiable newborn, Jasper does his best to resist her urges, and fails. Miserably and repeatedly, much to my delight. Dirty, Sexy, Unf."

With smut, the stories eliminate abstinence altogether. In "Never Sleep in a Strange Man's Bed," Bella, a human chef from Seattle visiting Hilton Head, North Carolina, has sex with Edward, a human architect, before she meets him in the light of day. They are irresistibly drawn together, but there is no presumption that sex will wait until marriage. Instead, they have to figure out how to make a long-distance relationship viable. In "The List," a fan favorite, Bella can do everything else except have sexual intercourse with Edward before they are married. The story is an interlude before their marriage in *Breaking Dawn,* and it treats readers to explicit sex scenes where she gives him a blow-job on their lab table at school or he makes her have an orgasm against the tree in her meadow. "I love fucking your mouth, Miss Swan. Now, come for me right now because I'm about to explode. *That did it.* Bella's muscles spasmed in a burst and she made a strangled noise around my cock. I hissed and pulled out as gently as I could manage and turned my hips away from her face just as my orgasm ripped through me and splattered to the floor. 'God damn fucking Christ, Bella!'" However, they wait until the wedding day for actual intercourse.

If fan fiction doesn't always adhere to virgin script, the most celebrated stories still make sure that Bella is fundamentally not "that kind of girl." She is never promiscuous, even if she does have a one-night stand with Edward. In the story "It Happened One Night," Bella is a graduate student who moonlights as a bartender in a club where Edward and Jasper frequently and indiscriminately pick up women. Edward, who works in an independent bookstore, immediately finds himself attracted to Bella at the expense of a brazen redhead modeled on Victoria, Bella's vampire nemesis in the actual series. They hook up that night and Bella feels "slutty." Yet Edward somehow instinctively knows, "She's not that girl, not one of those barflies who pick up a different guy to sleep with every weekend." Or, "She's giving in to something that she usually spends a lot of energy resisting. I'm momentarily stunned that she came home with me at all—I shouldn't brag about Bella like some sort of conquest when I know how hard it was for her to give in to that. The least I can do is respect her in that sense."

This same logic adheres to the Bella of canon Twilight. She may want more sex from Edward, but she's never a "bad girl" because she's still a virgin, innocent and deeply in love. Even Bella's sexual desire in Twilight is always conjoined with romantic love. Once she becomes an exquisitely beautiful vampire, what is it that Bella will be able to do? Discern the future like Alice? Read minds like Edward? Alter the mood in a room like Jasper? Have supernatural sex all day? No, Bella's sole desire is only to be able to find a way to love Edward more. "I would probably never be able to do anything interesting or special like Edward, Alice, and Jasper could do," she says in *Breaking Dawn*. "Maybe I would just love Edward more than anyone in the history of the world had ever loved anyone else. I could live with that."

In the Twilight books and WussPerv stories, it is purity in some form that guarantees the heroine romance. This is underscored by Edward's refusal to do more than kiss Bella until they are married. His rationale is that, in his own time, he would have asked permission from Bella's father to court her, stealing kisses with her while drinking lemonade on the front porch. WussPerv stories, like many romance novels, assume that the hero, rake, pirate, rapscallion, or womanizer only requires one instance with the awkward virgin or sexually inexperienced heroine to realize he has been completely tamed and that no one else will ever do for him. True love inevitably follows. The women who run the irreverent website *Smart Bitches, Trashy Books* have dubbed this the "Magic Hoo Hoo Theory."[15] The "orgasm of perfection means that she has inspired an intensity that's part obsession, part irritation and part priapism: he's hard for her, exclusively her, forever," they write. "Her magic Hoo Hoo brings him to monogamous attachment."[16] The Bella in "Master of the Universe" is tentative about becoming Edward's bondage slave but is also irresistibly drawn to him. Unsurprisingly, Edward turns out to harbor deep-seated issues with abandonment and abuse, comes to grip with them and his love for Bella, and relinquishes his need to be a dominator, and he and Bella end up in a consensual, multiple-orgasm-producing relationship. Rather than force her to submit to brutality or degradation, he breaks his own rules by being careful of her virginity, having "vanilla sex," and eventually insisting on marriage. As one reader commented on Twilighted.net, "I also think that maybe taking her virginity tied her more to him—he did keep telling her over and over, 'You are mine.'"

Both Twilight and WussPerv smut offer a romantic-boyfriend story in sharp contrast to the casual sex and heavy drinking endemic to some high schools and college campuses. Twilight Bella knows that the person to whom she loses her virginity truly loves her. As she hides in the bathroom on her honeymoon night in this scene from *Breaking Dawn*, she asks herself:

> How did people do this—swallow all their fears and trust someone else so implicitly with every imperfection and fear they had—with less than the absolute commitment that Edward had given me? If it weren't Edward out there, if I didn't know in every cell of my body that he loved me as much as I loved him—unconditionally and irrevocably and, to be honest, irrationally—I'd never be able to get up off this floor.

In her response to my survey, one fan talked about how she used the text as she contemplated her quandary about whether to have sex with her boyfriend: "It does affect what I think is love and makes me hold out for somebody that makes me feel the same way Bella does about Edward."

WussPerv stories also present the possibility of experiencing romantic fulfillment *and* erotic surrender. Whether it's the one night hook-up between Bella, the bartender and Edward, the philanderer; the long-distance relationship between Bella the chef and Edward the noncommittal architect; or the BDSM (bondage and discipline/dominance and submission/sadism and masochism) relationship between Bella the potential submissive and Edward the bondage master, each of their relationships evolve into those of true love, monogamy, and marriage.

In her book *Sex and the Soul*, Donna Freitas documents the dominance of "hook-up culture" after surveying thousands of students at religious and secular colleges and universities.[17] In this sexual milieu, some young women and men no longer date but instead meet for casual sex often fueled by alcohol. The time constraints of studying, work, and college life mean it is more "efficient" to hook up occasionally. The backdrop for hook-ups often feature disturbing theme parties like "CEOs and Hos," "Maids and Millionaires" "professors and schoolgirls," and "jock pros and sport hos," where men are the CEOs, millionaires, professors, and pros, and women are simply expected to show up wearing as little as possible. Freitas notes that these predominantly male, heterosexual fantasies mirror the scenarios of heterosexual pornography, which anyone can easily access on the Internet and which most young men admit to viewing or using well before they're adults.[18] Instead of watching online, hook-up culture enables the men to enact pornographic scenarios in everyday life.

Freitas finds that many women and some men are discontented with the dominance of hook-up culture, in which women are vilified for being virgins and for being sluts, and men are expected to sleep around.[19] One young woman learned that a soccer player she thought she was dating was actually taking bets from his team about whether he'd be the first to have sexual intercourse with her. Twilight's overlapping ideas about sexuality reflect and invert these broader and often pernicious norms about sex, particularly for girls and young women, in which the labels of bad or good girl, the slut or virgin, easy or virtuous are always shifting.[20] Contemporary girls and young women know that "what kind of girl" they are has a lot to do with sex, but the sexual rules are much less clear. As Amy Wilkins writes in her book about teenage Goths and Christians, "Gone are the days when good girls 'don't' and bad girls 'do.' Now good girls might, sometimes, depending on their feelings for the guy and who the guy is. Good girls, according to current cultural norms, should be concerned with how they look and express interest in boys, and they probably shouldn't be too uptight about sex. And aren't girls supposed to want to get their needs met, at least a little, too?"[21]

College students told Freitas that the term "yes girls" connotes a girl who hooks up too much; but if a girl opts out of sex, she's a prude. These rules, murky as they are, can also backfire. Girls can end up pregnant, they can inadvertently cross the slippery boundary between "hot" and "slutty," and they can be victimized and subsequently blamed for it.[22] In most fan-fic smut, romance fiction or paranormals, there are no repercussions for men as womanizers, serial daters, bondage masters, or general cads. The sexualization of young women, and the sexual cultures on some campuses and increasingly in high school, means that girls must navigate these nebulous double standards.

In November 2011, the American Association of University Women published a report based on a national survey that almost half of seventh- to twelfth-graders experienced sexual harassment in 2010–2011.[23] Girls were more likely to be subject to harassment, and one ninth-grade girl said, "I was called a whore because I have many friends that are boys." Figuring out how to follow the rules can bring respect, status, and protection from peers and adults; it can also mean that girls' own sexual desires and priorities take a backburner to the desires and perspectives of boys and/or adults. Sharon Thompson, the author of *Going All the Way*, interviewed hundreds of girls, and writes that, faced with a diminished investment in romance by boys, girls appear to make up the "love deficit" by offering sex, experienced often as pain, not pleasure, but as proof that the relationship is loving and meaningful.[24]

While hook-up culture certainly exists, it's questionable whether it is the epidemic that so many critics bewail. Also, not all young women abhor the idea of casual sex. Take the case of Karen Owen, a student at Duke University. In 2010, she created a fake thesis in the form of a PowerPoint presentation that explicitly rated the sexual prowess and penis size of male students, mainly athletes with whom she had sex. The site ignited an uproar when it went viral because it upended some cultural expectations of women as victims of hook-up culture.

What of romance? Freitas found that the way women understood romance was not dinners, beach walks, or even a piano-playing vampire serenading you but "just talking."[25] "We went for a walk on a warm evening, sitting and talking in a café for seven hours" is one among dozens of examples in which female students distinguish romance from sexual intimacy. In a discussion I had with college students about Twilight, many spoke with real longing of wanting their boyfriends to sneak into their rooms like Edward and merely hang out together, cuddling and talking. For many fans, the most romantic scene in *Twilight* the movie is when Edward and Bella huddle together on moss in the rain forest, deep in conversation.

If sex is a casual experience divorced from intimacy and dating, it's no wonder that Twilight and WussPerv smut captivate readers. For girls who are bombarded by injunctions against premarital sex from schools, churches, and parents, but witness promiscuity in everything from popular culture to the behavior of their own friends, the old-fashioned courtship of the Twilight fable is a relief and a fantasy. Fans in my survey admire Edward for his protectiveness and restraint: "I love the fact that he is such a gentleman and demonstrates enormous control when around her because he loves her when most would have just given in to temptation." They tended to focus on how Edward is from "an older time where you didn't take advantage of women." As the mother of a Twilight fan and a fan herself explained to a group at the Summer School in Forks symposium, "I tell [my daughter] just keep yourself pure and clean 'cause there's someone special out there just like Edward for everyone and you've just got to find him." Like this woman, other mothers and girls still harbor faith in the idea that out of an archaic and mystical code of honor, boys will protect their daughters rather than invite them to a party for "CEOs and Hos."

Hannah had told me back at TwiCon that "you got married after you held hands. You should be able to say no and have it be okay." Lara, the willowy honors student I also met at Twicon after our aerobics class, described losing her virginity as a tale of woe. "I don't know. I can think back to my very first boyfriend, and he was the wrong guy. At the time, you know, you can't see the forest for the trees. And we were, you know, pretty heavy." He ended up dumping her immediately after they'd had sex in high school, and she refused to date anyone else for fear she would get a reputation. The fairy tale of Bella and Edward in Twilight or WussPerv smut is mesmerizing given what is realistic sex for some young women and girls. Both constitute forms of romance porn written by women for female readers that allows them to have it all: smut, respect, and true love.

The Appeal of Fifty

If teenage girls have too little pleasure, too few options, and not enough sexual power, as scholars of girlhood and sexuality argue, does Twilight present an alternative? Bella might receive love and sex, safety and danger, but there is still no pleasure without penalty. Before the sex can be mind-blowing, before you can be married eternally as a vampire wife, the Twilight canon tells girls to expect some repercussions. In *Breaking Dawn*, when Bella and Edward finally have sex on their honeymoon, Bella awakens with bruises flowering across her body, a broken headboard, and drifting feathers from the pillow Edward has ripped with his teeth. Edward is chastened and worried, but Bella protests that she relished the experience and demands more, though he resists and decides they won't have sex again until she is a vampire. In response to her pleading, he tells her, "Maybe it would be more polite to wait until we're alone. *You* may not notice me tearing the furniture apart, but it would probably scare them," referring to the man and woman cleaning their honeymoon cottage. Edward may hurt Bella, but it's only because he can't control the floodgates of passion and lust, and those urges are tempered by his abiding love and self-loathing for battering her. Within a few weeks, she is saddled with a rib-cracking pregnancy and teenage motherhood.

I've seen many girls wearing the t-shirt that reads "Why Am I Covered in Feathers?" or "Edward can bust my headboard, bite my pillows, and bruise my body any day," pieces of Twilight merchandise that encapsulate the often contradictory portrayal of sexuality as both satisfying and damaging. One girl nonchalantly informed me on our van tour of Forks that the latter quote served as her Facebook status for weeks. When her uncle wrote in alarm to her parents after seeing her page, she simply responded that he shouldn't worry because she was referring to Edward, her fictional boyfriend. She told him, "Especially as teenage girls, we don't have the experience in this stuff."

Stephenie Meyer refrains from any description of sex throughout the canon, citing her own LDS beliefs and her concern that there is an excessive amount of attention to sex in contemporary literature. Therefore, the blank space between when they go to bed on their honeymoon and wake up to black-and-blue bodies, becomes the tabula rasa for girls and women to project their own fantasies of sex and romance. The only time the Twilight canon offers explicit description in relation to sex is when it concerns the pain involved. There are a lot of contusions but not many scenes of pleasure. The girl on Facebook isn't deluded into thinking that all sex comes with abuse, but she felt that this might be acceptable collateral damage for romance and eternal love.

Aside from the sex, the bondage relationship Edward desires in "Master of the Universe" is not so far removed from the relationship he has with Bella in the actual Twilight saga. Smut Bella must sign a contract in which she promises obedience: "The Submissive will obey any instructions given by The Dominant immediately without hesitation or reservation and in an expeditious manner." The contract includes exacting standards for sleeping, eating, dressing, exercising, and personal hygiene. Smut Edward also provides guidelines on her personal safety: "The Submissive will not drink to excess, smoke, take recreational drugs, or put herself in any unnecessary danger." It ends with the stipulation that

> The Submissive will not enter into any sexual relations with anyone other than The Dominant. The Submissive will conduct herself in a respectful and modest manner at all times. She must recognize that her behavior is a direct reflection on

The Dominant. She shall be held accountable for any mis-
deeds, wrongdoings, and misbehavior committed when not
in the presence of the Dominant. Failure to comply with any
of the above will be result in immediate punishment, the nature of which shall be determined by The Dominant.

Although obviously an exaggeration, this dynamic mirrors Bella and
Edward's often controlling and obsessive relationship throughout
the actual Twilight series. He spies on her, forbids her from visiting
Jacob or the woods, isolates her from her friends, dismantles her car,
and has his sister kidnap her for the weekend.

Meyer's lack of sexual description is compensated for in the thousands of smut Twilight stories in which the sex can be rough, tender
and erotic, gay and straight, all-human or not. Smut provides a broad
spectrum of sexual fantasy, and there is something for every reader.
It might not always be realistic, but at least it's explicit.

Fan fiction can also veer into extreme territory, with stories of
rape, incest, bondage, and sadomasochistic sex. In "The Submissive,"
Edward lashes a crying Bella twenty times. The tagline for the story
reads, "Can Bella Swan warm and win the heart of DOM, Edward
Cullen, while living out her darkest fantasy?" One fan writes on the
site, "I made the fatal error of first reading this tale in between meetings the other day. The subsequent meetings were NOT productive
as feck-me hot-to-trot Dom Edward Cullen was dominating my
mind (& lady crackers)." At the fan-fiction workshop I'm attending,
PsyMom differentiates between "clean smut" and "hardcore," and remarks that the genre of fan fiction is constantly shifting. Until 2007,
she argues, smut tended more toward the WussPerv, but now there
are stories with slash and more graphic violence and sex. She predicts
that the trend will reverse itself and return to what she considers
sweeter forms of smut because there is so much hardcore out there.

Awkward pauses and silences follow one woman's tentative
mention of "rape fic" in our workshop, and PsyMom's immediate response is that it "irritates" her. PsyMom draws a line against
that type of story, asserting that you won't find rape-fic stories on
Twilighted.net. If there are stories on the site containing sexual vio-

lence and abuse, Twilighted.net doesn't condone it but may allow it if it's done in context and is necessary for the character or plot. "We take it seriously," PsyMom says.

People are reading rape-fic, although the stories aren't featured in the top-ten lists, and it's ludicrous to think Twilighted.net can adjudicate what kinds of sexual fantasies should appeal to readers. It's not as if there isn't violence in Twilight, with Jacob forcibly kissing Bella or Edward manhandling her. The entire genre of romance fiction throughout the 1970s and 1980s, beginning with Kathleen Woodiwiss's *The Flame and the Flower*, the first single-title romance novel to be published as an original paperback in the United States, revolved around the idea that a heroine's first time with the hero is a non-consensual rape scene. Even as the heroine fights and cries, the hero is powerless to stop himself. What was so egregious about these books is that the woman eventually falls in love with her rapist. It was the central conceit of the genre until the 1990s, when other narratives and writers began to flourish.[26]

Yet, readers readily forgive the violent hero. The more tortured, tormented, and damaged the male character in Twilight or fan-fic, the more appealing he is, and the more fans sympathize with his occasional bouts of violence, possessiveness, manipulation, and general psychopathic behavior. These vampires' prodigious wealth, beauty, and immortality may separate them from mere humans, but in their self-scrutiny, they are also objects of sympathy. Edward is the ultimate romantic hero because he not only loves Bella but also loves her enough to deny his blood-thirsty vampire nature and to insist on marriage. One woman at the fan-fic workshop told me, "The part that is most appealing to me is that Edward has to be overly careful with her, even though he may not want to be. The temptation is so great, but he forces himself to resist." As Bella tells Edward in *Twilight*, "You're dangerous? . . . But not bad. . . . No, I don't believe that you're bad." The contemporary vampire in young adult and paranormal romance literature has become the slate upon which some women's desires for illicit sexuality and the safety of romance are projected.

As Ken Gelder argues in *Reading the Vampire*, vampires historically have represented collective anxieties about colonialism, otherness, capitalism, and contagion.[27] Or the vampire animates the unspeakable and brings to life as vampiric that which can't be named as otherwise.[28] Unlike the pure evil of Dracula or Nosferatu, in Edward and the vampire heroes of *True Blood* or *The Vampire Diaries*, we have the twenty-first-century, therapeutic vampire boyfriend. Desperate to retain their humanity and angst-ridden about their bloodthirsty natures, these vamps personify both danger and safety. Ananya Mukherjea writes that the agony the contemporary vampire of young adult literature has regarding his vampiric nature may also be compelling because it represents "the dissatisfaction that many heterosexually involved women would like to see their male partners feel about their own gendered dominance."[29] Even the evil vampires in *Twilight* and other current young adult books who have no scruples about consuming human blood undergo various forms of self-analysis. Their desire for redemption is, after all, a perennially romantic idea.

The Edward of smut fan-fic is an iteration of the romance-novel hero, brooding and wounded, damaged but essentially good—in addition to being a stunning physical specimen of virility. The adjectives that describe him are also rampant clichés in romance literature: steely eyes, washboard abdomens, midnight hair, prominent brows, and hawk-like noses. At the Fade to Black workshop, Twilightzoner and others are self-deprecatingly aware that these male characters are archetypes far removed from their lives. PsyMom asked rhetorically, "What would we do with a husband if he looked like Edward? If he looked like Emmett?" Without missing a beat, Twilightzoner replied, "We'd get plastic surgery."

At the workshop, there are wisecracks about "Sullen Edward Cullen" and his endless angst and tortured soul. Smut Edward, human or vampire, also often personifies the conflicted hero. Fans nicknamed the bondage Edward in "Master of the Universe" Fifty because he is "fifty shades of fucked up." Surprise, surprise, Edward has a troubled past. There are his profound issues with food and being touched. His first sexual relationship was as a submissive to a much older woman, whom Bella calls "Mrs. Robinson." Edward appears to be ruthless and calculating, but underneath, awakened by the love of Bella, is a man who was abused as a boy and left to rot in foster care. Only the realization of his love for Bella helps him to forsake the violent parts of his past. One reader on Twilighted .net noted, "[Edward] seems to be aching for real human connection yet completely inept at understanding how that happens? That prior to Bella, it seems he has NEVER achieved the intimacy of sex with someone with whom he had an emotional connection. . . . I see a very damaged, very good hearted man trying his best to convince himself that he is the master of his universe."

Readers maintain deep emotional investments in the fan-fic wounded Edward. One "MofU" reader expressed a revolution in her feelings toward smut Edward when he became Fifty. "I wanted to break down that control[led] facade and see him smile. Yet, I also started liking his dominance. It was sexy, and his playroom was nice. Not that I'd want canes and clamps either, but it seemed Bella wasn't complaining too much." This same woman joked that Fifty became so real to her that she would tweet about him with a friend, especially regarding his obsession about finishing food. "One day I didn't finish my lunch because it tasted nasty. I threw it away, but I tweeted that I was afraid Fifty would find out and yell at me for being wasteful. He is written so well that he will stick with you."

Smut may lack Twilight's titillating fantasy of deferred sexuality, but smut compensates with the grittiness of sex in abundance. Fans crave both the abstinence porn and the smut, which is why they veer from the canon to fan-fiction and back again. It bespeaks the endurance of the desire for a dangerous sexual predator and chivalrous suitor, and how this fantasy seeps into everyday life. Someone in the workshop mentioned a newspaper article about a seventeen-year-old Michigan girl at the film premiere of *New Moon*. Upon emerging from the theater, she told a police officer that a man sitting near her had bitten her on the neck and assaulted her in the parking lot.[30] Her story later proved to be untrue. . . . Upon hearing the story, Twilightzoner retorted, "She should have been reading smut."

Breaking Dawn

"Why am I covered in feathers?" I asked, confused.
He exhaled impatiently. "I bit a pillow. Or two . . ."

After three long books and films full of heated glances and close-ups of Bella biting her lip and Edward staring at her with a mix of gloom and lust, we finally get sex and a wedding. Bella and Edward marry right after high school graduation. In the film (*Breaking Dawn–Part I*), the Cullens effortlessly heft tree trunks over their shoulders as part of the pre-wedding preparations. Bella cautiously plods down the aisle in a fabulously elegant wedding dress, designed for the film by Carolina Herrera, and implores her dad, "Don't let me fall." (Fans anticipated this dress for months, and once the film was released, knockoffs went on sale everywhere. There is even a website that features Bella and Edward–themed weddings.) Bella approaches Edward, the groom, while clusters of what appear to be sinuous ivory tinsel dangle from trees. The camera swoops around them as they state their vows, and then there is a kiss that goes on forever.

There is a montage of wedding toasts, including one from Edward's vampire brother Emmett, who warns Bella, "You won't be getting a lot of sleep."

Earlier, when Edward wants to come clean about his past of eating humans (he only ate men he knew were murderers of women) and warns Bella that he has something to tell her, she replies, "What, you're not a virgin?"

Jacob crashes the wedding. Bella is thrilled to see him, but he threatens to disrupt things when he learns that Edward and Bella plan to try to consummate their marriage while she's still human. Jacob growls at Edward that he'll kill her without anyone specifically uttering the word sex. Before a brawl erupts, the Quileute wolf pack materializes from the woods to stop Jacob. Bella and Edward drive off in Edward's super-shiny Volvo for their surprise honeymoon destination.

In the film, we're supposed to know we're in Rio de Janeiro because Bella and Edward watch Brazilians dancing and grinding in the street while musicians play. On an island off the coast, which Carlisle purchased and named for his wife, Esme, Edward and Bella finally have sex. His hand grips the headboard of their bed, and it shatters during the act.

The next morning, Bella is covered in bruises but begs for more because the sex was perfect. The book is more explicit in describing how she wakes black and blue, but in the film, she merely has a few faint marks. Someone watching the film next to me muttered, "Right, because your first time is always so wonderful."

Edward refuses to do it again because of his fear of hurting her, but he succumbs one more time when Bella awakes weeping and begging him. What happens after sex? Bella becomes pregnant with a vampire/human hybrid baby who reaches full-term by four weeks, cracks her ribs, and inhabits Bella's body like a succubus. They rush home to Forks so Carlisle can aid them.

The fetus is incompatible with Bella's body, and as it grows, she withers to an emaciated skeletal figure with a giant belly. Yet Bella willingly sacrifices herself for the baby. Her transformation from skittish bride to gaunt shell is complete. Jacob and Edward reach a manly truce to protect Bella's wasted frame just as Rosalie vigilantly becomes Bella's bodyguard against all the men around her who want her to abort the baby in order to save her own life. "It's a baby," Rosalie growls when someone refers to the unborn child as "it" or "the fetus." Once Edward can hear the baby's voice in Bella's belly, he stops pushing for an abortion and begins to feel tenderness for the baby. To placate the fetus, whom they call Renesmee, a combination of Bella's and Edward's mothers' names, Bella sips blood through a straw in a cup.

During the birth, Jacob shows up, irate and threatening Edward as usual. When he's not growling jealously, he's making sarcastic comments. Jacob breaks from his pack in order to protect Bella in the most hilarious scene in the film where the computer-generated wolves pace and argue with each other over what to do about the "mutant" baby that Bella is carrying. Just as the wolf pack starts to descend in order to kill Bella, the baby breaks Bella's spine.

> Another shattering crack inside her body, the loudest yet . . . Her legs, which had been curled up in agony, now went limp, sprawling out in an unnatural way.
> "Her spine," [Edward] choked in horror.

Carlisle diverts the wolf pack away from Bella while Edward and Jacob perform a gory emergency caesarean section, which entails Edward biting into Bella's uterus. When the baby emerges, Edward gazes adoringly at her, while presumably Bella's entrails are spilling out. The next thing you know, Jacob looks intently into the baby's eyes and envisions her growing up to become a nubile teenager, when she'll be joined to him for life. She's been imprinted.

To save Bella's life, Edward transforms her into a vampire by injecting her with his venom through a giant needle in her chest and biting her all over. After the gruesome C-section, Bella begins her metamorphosis into a voluptuous vampire with luscious hair and shimmering eye shadow, an extra benefit of vampire transformation. Everyone comments over and over on how beautiful she's become. "The way everyone looked at me made me uncomfortable," she says. "Even Edward. It was like I had grown a hundred feet during the course of the morning. I tried to ignore the impressed looks, mostly keeping my eyes on Nessie's sleeping face and Jacob's unchanged expression." Forsaking her parents, friends, and a mortal life is worth it because now she's perfect and beautiful, and she has a baby, nicknamed Nessie, who will grow to be seventeen and never age a year after that. And Nessie can spend her eternity with Jacob, her imprinter, until he presumably grows old.

Of course, Bella adjusts remarkably well to vampirehood without the usual nasty side effect of being a blood-crazed newbie, and she successfully wears a cocktail dress on her first animal hunt. We still don't get any explicit sex, but we learn that she and Edward never tire of confessing how much they love each other. Even her voice is more melodic post-transition. In *Breaking Dawn*, Bella says:

> I made a concerted effort to focus. There was something I needed to say. The most important thing. . . . "I love you," I said, but it sounded like singing. My voice rang and shimmered like a bell. . . . "As I love you," he told me.

Knowing that Nessie is a rare vampire/human hybrid, the Volturi return from Italy, presumably to snatch her away and bring her back to their vampire citadel. Vampire allies gather in Forks to support the Cullens, and we anticipate blood, gore, and an epic battle of good versus evil, but nothing happens except some arguing and mind-control. Everyone, except secondary vampire characters we never knew, goes home unscathed. Edward and Bella continue "blissfully into this small but perfect piece of our forever."

CHAPTER 5

Where to Spend
Those Twilight Dollars

I'm lurking outside the Pendragon booth, whose primary wares consist of Renaissance fair–style gowns with cleavage-baring bodices. The clothes resemble a cross between retro-medieval and S&M bondage. While it's unlikely that I could bring myself to wear a purple leather bustier with dangling straps that cinch across the chest, plenty of others congregate in the booth apparently in search of just that sort of clothing. Pendragon is among the half dozen vendors arrayed in the hall for the official Twilight Convention in Burlingame, California, one of approximately twenty conventions organized by Creation Entertainment that are conducted around the country. Here, local fans might glimpse and obtain an autograph from the actors who play the Quileute wolf pack or Cullen vampires, listen to semifamous fan-site webmistresses, and amass Twilight merchandise. Creation Entertainment knows that the danger for fans arises when, without another book to read, life begins to feel barren. Fans want to prolong the experience. The swoon-inducing possibility of celebrity proximity and the desire for the next Twilight product, like the dinnerware from Bella's wedding or a Cullen throw blanket, sustain fans in the months of drought between a new film or significant fanpire gossip ("Is Stephenie really writing a new novel?!"; "Rob and Kristen finally came clean and are really dating!"; "Kristen Stewart expecting first child, not a vampire!").

Alphie and Pel, the women who helm the famous *Twilight Lexicon* fan site, are currently fawning over Pendragon's clothes. Pel, a

New Jersey resident with a penchant for emphasizing her Bronx roots, holds up a velvet serving-wench-style dress, while Alphie, her dimples flashing as she laughs, gestures that it's too long. I'm hovering as I debate whether to approach them for an interview. I'd met Alphie over a year ago at the Summer School in Forks when I was a relative Twilight newbie and hadn't yet learned the hierarchy of fan sites within the Twilight firmament. Later, when I sent a deferential e-mail asking if they'd talk to me, they explained that they only cooperate with projects approved by the Hachette Book Group, the publisher for Meyer's books. This time, I thought I could perhaps ingratiate myself through common ground. I know they are die-hard Jane Austen fans like me. They've read the Black Dagger Brotherhood series and gone to book signings, and I made it through most of the series. We're the same age. We all have kids. I lived in New Jersey, too. I can keep my aversion to Pendragon's clothes to myself. Still, I wait to approach them.

Presiding over the fanpire as gatekeepers and tastemakers, Alphie, the site's founder, is Lori Joffs, and Pel, co-owner and writer of most of the daily news on the site, is Laura Byrne-Cristiano. The *Twilight Lexicon* is the oldest, perhaps most widely read, and certainly most influential fan site. Their endorsement of an event, blog, or product potentially reaches and sways thousands of fans. Alphie and Pel reign at the apex of the Twilight fanpire partially because of their friendship with Stephenie Meyer, who crowned their site "the brightest star in the Twilight universe." Their chummy relationship with Summit Entertainment also supplies them with invitations to red-carpet premieres and coveted knowledge about everything Twilight-related.

Alphie visited the film sets of *Twilight* and *New Moon* and interviewed Taylor Lautner, Kristen Stewart, and Robert Pattinson live. Pel's online bio states, "She notably debunked the Vanessa Hudgens casting, and Stephenie Meyer lawsuit rumors ahead of major media." Pel "routinely connects with representatives from EW, Access Hollywood, and EXTRA to name a few." Alone or together, the *Lexicon* women appear at most Creation Entertainment–sponsored events. They refused to attend TwiCon because they doubted the professionalism of the organizers. In an e-mail, they explained to me that they are not paid to attend the conventions but travel expenses are "picked up" in exchange for their presentations and help, something that more amateur and less advertiser-driven sites wouldn't be able to achieve.[1] The *Lexicon* does advertise the Creation Entertainment conventions, however. As Pel put it, "I suspect [Creation Entertainment] enjoys working with us because we put out a quality product in a professional and timely manner that targets their demographic, and the coverage/access at their events is mutually beneficial." With the *Lexicon*, the distinction between business brand strategy and personal identity construction in digital spaces has collapsed. What does it mean to be a fan when the fan activities aren't as much about individual tastes or even belonging to a community, but rather about fans laboring in the name of the self-brand like the *Lexicon* and a company brand like Summit?

Alphie and Pel are featured speakers at this convention, celebrities by their proximity to Meyer and their insider knowledge of the books and films. They are the closest thing to Twilight royalty.

❧

As its name suggests, the *Twilight Lexicon* was designed to provide a catalogue or information source for all things Twilight, including vampire lore and the public offices of Forks, Washington, to detailed chapter summaries, character biographies, and a series timeline. "If there is a quote from the book she can tell you exactly where it is located on the page having practically a photographic memory," reads Alphie's bio. Alphie met Pel on a fan site for Remus Lupin of Harry Potter. Alphie "got her into Twilight by nagging and begging for someone else to read it," because Pel harbors an aversion to vampire stories. In addition to Remus, they possess a mutual love of amateur theatre and singing. The *Lexicon* now receives approximately thirty thousand unique hits a day.

Their fame and lack of approachability is based on their authenticity. They were there, way back in March 2006, a vaunted golden age when Stephenie Meyer still visited local libraries, logged on to fan forums like *TwilightMoms*, kept a MySpace page, and interacted with fans at book signings. In a fan flashback series, one woman waxed nostalgic about this innocent period "when Stephenie still had the 'Contact' option on her website." The woman wrote Meyer "gushing over my love for the series" and asking when she would release *New Moon*. She cherishes Meyer's response: "It was cool to hear from people who liked the books." The *Lexicon* even has a feature called "Fandom Flashbacks," harkening back to the early days of the fandom five years ago, a lifetime in fandom years. It allows fans "to take a peek at some of the things you might have missed along the way," such as early book signings with Meyer and the small gatherings known as "I Love Edward Cullen" parties.

By many accounts, Meyer remains down-to-earth, despite curtailing fan communication. At the *Twilight* film premiere, after talking to MTV, she deliberately snubbed the mainstream press to give fan-site creators first dibs on interviews. Yet, the town of Forks has repeatedly beseeched her to send a statement for their annual Stephenie Meyer Day celebration, and her publicist always turns them down. When their crumbling high school was being rebuilt, they needed around $200,000 to save and restore the original 1925 facade but were unable to raise the funds. Neither Meyer nor Summit Entertainment, with the millions in profit from Twilight, has ever donated money to Forks.

Back in those pre-celebrity days, Stephenie Meyer read fan fiction. In 2006, the website Fanfiction.net had no Twilight section (now it's the largest fan-fiction section out there, aside from Harry Potter), and Alphie posted a story, only one of thirty about Twilight, that narrated the series from Edward's point of view. Meyer actually read it and e-mailed her. Alphie was "all nervous" when they spoke on the phone, according to her recollection on the *Twilight Lexicon*. They discovered that before Meyer became one of the hundred most influential people in the world, according to *Time* magazine, she actually shared a lot in common with Alphie. They are the same age with the same number of kids and both are members of the LDS Church. At a book exposition in Washington, DC, Alphie and Pel arranged to have dinner with Meyer, and caught up again at Meyer's book signings in Texas and Nashville. According to Alphie, a lively correspondence ensued in which Meyer granted Alphie her imprimatur to create a lexicon. Alphie became Meyer's default editorial assistant as well, checking for consistencies in all the books and reading book drafts months before they went to her publisher.

The *Lexicon* women embody the shifts in the fanpire from independent conventions to corporate juggernaut and from do-it-yourself blogging to vetted celebrity. Consumerism and self-invention are intertwined in the inevitable megacommercialization of Twilight. It's a part of the romance of Twilight in the age of mundane celebrity: everyone wants to be one and be close to one. Stargazing and plotting your own social-media debut, as well as the thrill of participation and the satisfaction of purchase, are ways to buy into the enchantment of Twilight and keep the Twilight universe enfolded into the fabric of everyday life. Kaleb Nation, founder of the *Twilight Guy* website, once referred to fans as an "army" storming bookstores, conventions, and movie theaters seeking connection, enchantment, and the next Robert Pattinson doll. The fans want the ineffable Twilight high to last as long as possible, and the corporate sponsors of these events are certainly delighted to oblige.

Promising a Fan-tastic Experience

Pel deliberates a bit more over the dress until she and Alphie break away in time to take the stage for their presentation. I continue to peruse the offerings in the narrow hall adjacent to the auditorium. Aside from Pendragon, there is a booth for Kimmy Makes Scents, perfumes designed by two women from Valencia, California, with names like Beloved, Bleeding Heart, and Imprint, "the perfect infusion of grassy fern and patchouli, this scent captures the image of running through the forest with the scents of fresh leaves and earth beneath your feet." Native Jewelry from Arizona sells necklaces and bracelets designed by Native Americans. Three giant tables sponsored by Creation/Summit Entertainment laden with t-shirts, official merchandise, and photos fans purchase for autographs command the rest of the space. Convention appears a bit of a misnomer for this event since the Twilight happenings are confined to this constricted space for the six vendors and an auditorium that seats approximately eight hundred. Each Creation-sponsored fan event unfailingly follows the same format, except during the weeks leading up to a film premiere: fans pay to sit in front of a central stage flanked by fake Olympic-peninsula evergreens and giant posters of the actors, while speakers emit the sounds of rain and thunder. Rotating *Twilight* film stills flit across the screen. Even though the auditorium is less than half full, I take my assigned seat in the dimly lit back row as I didn't pay for a premium seat.

This particular TwiTour bills itself as taking place in San Francisco, but it's actually being held south of the city in the suburb of Burlingame, a forty-minute train ride away. The Hyatt Regency is a rather generic hotel, but I know I've passed into Twilight territory when I see a string of girls between sixteen and twenty clad in Twilight-slogan t-shirts in line to register. Handing out tickets is an affable, tall, ghostly pale, twentysomething guy with black gelled hair, rubber earrings, and a black suit with a silver tie. This lesser Edward Cullen or erstwhile vampire banters with the fans awaiting entrance, a more diverse group than I've seen at the Dallas or Utah conventions, due, no doubt, to the fact that it's being held in the Bay Area. The one factor uniting all the attendees here is the ubiquity of black jeans and twilight gray or black shirts; multiple earrings; and hair dyed black or bleached, which reflects the Goth-meets-suburbia aesthetics of the fanpire and the pervasive uniform of American youth. One girl's t-shirt reads, "Stupid Lamb."

In August 2009, Summit Entertainment, producer of the Twilight films, formed a partnership with Creation, who has been in the business of running conventions since 1971 when Star Trek was the phenomenon of choice. Their tagline for Twilight fans is "Come and experience a *fan*tastic weekend you'll never forget!" Their press release promises that the gatherings will feature Twilight celebrities, exclusive footage screenings, theme parties, musical performances, costume competitions, auctions, autographs, and merchandising and photo opportunities. Erin Ferries, the vice president of Creation, sought to dispel the idea that the conventions are just about money in a press release: "While the conventions will offer fans the chance to cheer for their favorite actors they are equally about gathering with like-minded folks and forming friendships based on a common devotion. We can't wait to bring some of the magic of TWILIGHT live to cities around the United States, Canada and the United Kingdom!" Nancy Kirkpatrick, the president of worldwide marketing for Summit Entertainment, added, "We wanted to find a way to allow them to immerse themselves in the films and the characters in a much more interactive setting. The Official TWILIGHT Fan Conventions will offer incredible opportunities to get up close to the characters which they have grown to love."[2]

Despite paeans to fan devotion and interaction, Gary Berman, the owner of Creation Entertainment, explains to me that his company's events are strictly about showbiz and are entertainment-oriented. When I mention TwiCon, he interjects impatiently that Twilight fans don't want to go to academic panels or self-defense classes. They're here to see Peter Facinelli, the actor who plays Carlisle, and obtain autographs. One of the main events at a Creation TwiTour consists of standing in an interminable line to request an autograph or picture with a member of the film cast, primed for that tantalizing moment of coming face-to-face with a wolf-pack member or Cullen vampire. As the newest and least famous cast members, the wolf-pack actors tend to show up for Creation conventions, though the Cullen vampires, with the exception of Facinelli, whose regular presence bespeaks his endless goodwill and patience, have stopped.

At a Creation convention held a year earlier, I noticed a pronounced hush in the usual din of the convention hall. A phalanx of burly men froze in front of me, encircling Kellan Lutz and Jackson Rathbone, the actors who play Edward's vampire brothers in the film and who are the objects of profuse fan adulation. If only Carly, who wore her "Carly Lutz. If found, please return to Kellan" button, were here, I thought. Kellan was mere inches from me, waiting for his escort to clear the path ahead. He glanced over at me with trepidation, as if I might attempt to leap into his arms, a valid fear as I'd heard that a fan had attempt this earlier. By the time I realized his identity, though, they were on the move again, the buzz induced by celebrity proximity hummed around me.

After the film clip, Jasper, or rather an impersonator who plays him at conventions as part of a paid act called the Hillywood Players, grabs the microphone to explain the rules of the convention. Sit in your assigned seat and no taking videos, only still pictures. If you want to interact with the people on stage like the *Lexicon* webmistresses or actors, there are question boxes outside. If part of what draws fans to Twilight is the way it fosters a sense of belonging, as the Summit executive wrote, it's odd how in the spaces where you might finally meet that online friend you've been joking with in a forum or interact with fellow fans, you can now only await an autograph, stare at the screen, or watch someone performing as the Twilight characters. This is a spectacle more conducive to slumber than celebration as you passively sit, ogle, and listen. Unlike the gleeful atmosphere of other fan events, at this Creation event, fans wait sedately, almost primly anticipating the first talk. In some ways, it's not even necessary to be physically present to get a sense of what is going on. The *Lexicon* regularly live tweets events—"Follow along with Pel at the San Fran TwiTour!"

This is more corporate, tame, regulated, and scripted than other fan events I've attended, and at the risk of indulging in the same fandom nostalgia I accused the *Lexicon* people of earlier, I find myself missing the zany aerobics, volleyball, layer cakes with scenes of Volterra, and Edward impersonators at TwiCon, Forks Summer School, and the *TwilightMoms'* Utah event. Despite the *Lexicon* hawking "gold pass giveaways" and discounted tickets to events, the fanpire doesn't universally endorse the TwiTours either. One sampling of complaints from attendees at the March 2011 Los Angeles convention on Goldstar.com, a site that provides tickets to various entertainment events, includes, "Hands down the worst convention of any kind I have ever heard of, much less attended. The $20 admission gave us access to a room with six vendors (not exaggerating). . . . I see more Twilight material in a Barnes & Noble than at this con. We literally finished the convention in 12 minutes. It was a pure scam." Another disparaged the convention, writing, "There wasn't much to see for it to be a 'Convention.' I was very disappointed because I am a very big fan of the Saga." In Forks, many local stores such as

Alice's Closet and Leppell's stock Twilight merchandise to assuage the Twilight tourists who throng the streets. Threatening letters from Summit's lawyers over their right to sell certain items that they deem the provenance of Summit's brand have hampered small retailers' ability to stay afloat and fueled the perception that Twilight profits take precedence over Twilight fans. One Forks merchant delighted in calling them "Scummit."

Where to Spend Those Twilight Dollars

The conventions are expensive, and one girl wrote on Goldstar.com that she was surprised about all the extra fees she had to pay to have her picture taken with a celebrity: "i did not take a picture with any of the special guests because i didn't come prepared to spend more money!! Overall, it was an ok event, I got to see Peter Facinelli which was cool, but i will not attend another event like this again, it is not worth it!"

Helpfully, the *Lexicon* has a post about how to attend a Twilight convention on a budget: "Is it possible to do a convention on a budget? The answer is yes. We'll show you how below." They break down the costs for fans: "If you go to the convention on a Saturday or Sunday on a general admission day pass, you usually end up seeing three stars minimum, do a Q & A, you get a Lexicon panel (sorry shameless self-promotion), a Hillywood panel, chance to win trivia/ costume contest prizes, and the ability to take as many pictures as you want of the celebrities onstage with your own camera, and you have access to the vendor room where you can drop more cash if you so choose." They explain how much more it costs to get an autograph ($25), a professional photo with you and an actor ($40), or a babysitter (free if the kids are under age six).

Unlike the Twilight Mom's Utah event, which benefits Alex's Lemonade Stand, or Twilight Fan Trips, which organize vampire baseball games in Salt Lake City and New Orleans for charity, Twi-Tours are purely profit-driven. When you play vampire baseball with actors like Peter Facinelli as part of the Fan Trips, up to 50 percent of net proceeds from each ticket helps specific local causes, such as rebuilding the thousand-seat football stadium at G.W. Carver Senior High School in New Orleans, which was destroyed during Hurricane Katrina.

Scholar Henry Jenkins calls some fandoms participatory cultures to describe how the social bonds and shared experiences of fandom engage the fanpire with other civic and political issues, creating a trajectory from popular media fandom to political engagement.[3] Out of Harry Potter–fan obsession emerged the Harry Potter Alliance, an organization with a mission to draw on the values of Harry Potter to instigate social change via what they call Dumbledore's Army.[4] If the books herald the rights of Muggles and wizards, of good over evil, so can fans. Fans in the Harry Potter Alliance campaigned for LGBT rights in Maine through a Wrock (Wizard Rock) concert, and knocked on doors and organized to raise money for earthquake survivors in Haiti. LeakyCon, the charity convention thrown by the staff of the Leaky Cauldron, the main Harry Potter fan site, has donated more than $20,000 to nonprofits over the past two years. The organizers wrote on their website, "We hope to use LeakyCon 2011 to render that figure minuscule."[5] At the Wrock for Equality event, fans aligned themselves with their favorite Hogwarts House and received points for every call made to a Maine voter. Celebrities from the fandom were appointed as the heads of each house since Maggie Smith and Alan Rickman were presumably not available. Harry Potter fans were drawn into this activism through "cocooning participants in successive layers of belonging."[6] They champion an issue with parallels to the book, identify with fictional characters, and surround themselves by like-minded readers. Aside from the charity baseball games, though, the themes of the Twilight books resist this kind of social justice identification, and burgeoning forms of participatory culture were entirely absent from the TwiTours.

⤜⤟

How to retain the enchanted feeling of being engulfed in a book series? Fans certainly attempt to replicate the blissful immersion of their first time read by rereading the series ten, fifteen, or thirty times. There is the giddiness of being surrounded by fans who are equally obsessed. The momentum of the fandom is shifting from the Twilight books to the films, as the producers tease fans with trailers and announcements of casting decisions. This inexorable commodification is wholeheartedly embraced by many fans, especially when they begin to feel Post-Saga Depression (PSD), the blue feeling that descends after finishing the books and realizing there is no actual Edward. You can also signal your affiliation with t-shirts, fangs, amber-colored contact lenses, or experience Alice's pixie nature embodied in a perfume, readily available in the vast, bazaar-like atmosphere online or at some conventions. Everything on display at official conventions is based on spinoff marketing, celebrity endorsement, and steering fans to other movies that feature the Twilight actors.

The fannish origins of a site like the *Twilight Lexicon* and its ascent into corporate sponsorship and semicelebrity status demonstrate how, as Matt Hills writes in his book on fan culture, it's now impossible to determine where grassroots culture ends and commercial culture begins.[7] According to Hills, the erosion of the distinction between popular and high culture, the changing relationship between physical and virtual spaces, the social interactions occurring in them, and the ways identities arise out of consumption and production mean that niche media has started to blend in to the mainstream.

"Cardio with the Cullens," vampire baseball, and celebrity autographs are part of a spectrum of commercialization. In an essay in the book *Bitten by Twilight*, Marianne Martens argues that the Twilight series is illustrative of a "two-tiered commodification."[8] She argues that publishers now think of books as transmedia products and focus on their earnings potential to the detriment of their literary value, while also commodifying fans by steering them to officially approved media. Even if Summit has a financial interest in convincing fans to attend conventions as long as possible and sell them everything from toothpaste to tiaras, pitting consumerism against community flattens the complexity of the fandom.

One way to prolong the Twilight sensation is through retail therapy Twilight-style. One vendor prominently displayed Sweethearts, a heart-shaped candy with the phrases "bite me" or "soul mate" on them and pictures of the actors on the cover of the container.

You could also buy *Female Force: Stephenie Meyer*, a comic-book retelling of the story of Meyer's life. Nordstrom sells an exclusive Twilight-inspired clothing line, including raincoats for inclement but vampire-friendly weather. There are the Twilight video game and Twilight Barbies. There are calendars, umbrellas, baseball bats, and shoelaces that say Team Jacob. For the bathroom, you might have Glow-In-The-Dark Edward Face Soap, Bella-inspired deodorant, or a tampon holder with Edward's head on the top. Never sleep alone again with the Manllow, an Edward-shaped pillow with arms that provide a cozy place to snuggle up at night. Or keep a life-size poster of him stationed at your bedside standing sentinel as you sleep. Do you want a cross-stitch pattern, a key chain, a pair of stockings or underwear with Edward's face on the crotch or with the line, "This ass belongs to Edward"? A shower curtain with a snarling werewolf on it? How about a reproduction of Bella's green flowered birthday dress in *New Moon*? Or a copy of her engagement ring?

Why be yourself when you can become Bella or Edward in a Twilight-themed photo shoot for proms and yearbook? Or you can name your child Bella (currently experiencing a rise in popularity according to the Social Security Administration, from the rank of 200 in 2007 to 58 in 2010).[9] The Vamp, a pale vibrator that sparkles, is aimed at the more adventurous and less young-adult demographic. According to the designers, you can

> toss it in the fridge for that authentic experience. The Vamp is a realistic form dildo based appropriately on our Sire's design but with a deathly pale flesh tone reminiscent of the new moon's glow. Don't be surprised if this toy seduces you, its long sleek shaft and deliciously ridged head calling to you in the twilight. But don't save this for just nocturnal escapades, try taking our Vamp out in the sunlight and watch him sparkle. Don't let this eclipse pass into the breaking dawn, place your order today.

For procreation, there are sperm banks that advertise donors who resemble Robert Pattinson.[10] Twilight reusable diapers and a car-seat cover that reads, "I drive like a Cullen" appeals to fans with children. Other, more R-rated products include condoms in a black wrapper, glitter lube, and a "sex necklace" featuring a picture of Bella straddling Edward.

I never saw the Vamp for sale at any conventions where the merchandise unabashedly targeted the coveted tween market. The discovery by advertisers and retailers that girls between eight and fourteen years of age have purchasing power through the largesse of their parents, has resuscitated the entire young-adult book industry and its spinoff entertainment. Parents and children now collectively decide how the family money is spent, and companies are eager to grab the attention of this highly coveted demographic. According to a recent report on tween spending, they wield $43 billion annually of their own funds derived from allowances, with parents spending an additional $170 billion on their kids.[11] Therefore, franchises like Twilight and Harry Potter desperately seek to create products that appeal to parents' desires for media entertainment like High School Musical or Twilight that is clean, empowering, and without explicit sexual content.

Then there is the stuff that Summit doesn't have a monopoly on. I've been collecting pictures of noncommercial Twilight fan creations for some time, and the sheer strangeness of some of them is mind-boggling and wonderful. Hands down, my favorite is "Bella's womb," shaped and textured like a hairy coconut sliced in half with Russian doll layers of red wool (blood) surrounding a nest of something resembling a Brillo pad cradling a small white figurine of a fetus. This is a lovingly constructed and creepy homage to Bella's uterus. Presumably, from this hirsute shell, Bella will birth Renesmee, a vampire-human hybrid with the fate of having her grandmothers' names combined. My runner-up in that category is the Twilight embryo Christmas ornament. And before the premiere of *New Moon*, someone plowed Edward's and Jacob's faces into a giant cornfield. A fan-designed "Cullen tree" has charms dangling from the ends of a whisk whose wires have been cut free and set in a glass jar filled with red, blue, and white beads. Each medallion or leaf contains the name of a character written in cursive with a quote on the back. Emmett's leaf, addressed to Bella, sardonically reads, "I'm really glad Edward didn't kill you. Everything's so much more fun with you around." At the convention, one fan wore spray-painted Converse high-tops with Edward's face and red laces that read, "You are my life now" in cursive. And then there is the annual pumpkin-carving contest, sponsored by the *Lexicon* and other fan sites. The runner-up had carved a lion, a lamb, and a heart on her jack-o'-lantern, but the winner was an elaborate wood-cut-like pumpkin replete with Jacob's face.

These quirky creations bespeak a reverence for Twilight that surpasses the purchase of a t-shirt. At a website devoted to Twilight tattoos, a trailing quote across one girl's collarbone reads, "Look after my heart. I've left it with you." These lines from *New Moon* cascade down another fan's entire upper back: "Time passes. Even when it seems impossible. Even when each tick of the second hand aches like the pulse of blood behind a bruise. It passes unevenly, in strange lurches and dragging lulls, but pass it does." By engraving Twilight on the body or changing their eye color with vampire contact lenses, fans initiate the process of perhaps morphing into something new, reborn, different from what they were before. They may not become exquisite vampires, but they can reside in a body transfigured, an incessant reminder inscribed in the flesh.

This longing for renewal and transportation into another world is the premise of *Lost in Austen*, a British TV series for which I share an affinity with Alphie and Pel of the *Lexicon*. In it, a modern London girl's obsession with *Pride and Prejudice*, combined with her disgruntlement with her boyfriend, helps her to pry open a portal in her bathroom that leads to the upstairs hall in Elizabeth Bennet's home. There she collides with Mr. Darcy and eventually trades places with Elizabeth, who gladly surrenders Darcy and rural 1820s England for short hair, iPods, and the independence of modern life. Isn't this the fantasy of every fan who is captivated by a particular story?

Stephenie Discovered Me

Within the fanpire, one might not only vicariously experience celebrity but also achieve it oneself. After all, who isn't enticed by the idea that from being a mere fan one could emerge a celebrity with sway over the rest of the fanpire? Beyond the girl with the tattoo reading, "There are no rules that can bind you when you find your other half," on her forearm, there is a whole stratum of fans who broke through and now receive accolades from other fans. The fanpire survives through websites, blogs, and social media platforms like Facebook and Twitter. Online, there are hundreds of fan websites and Facebook groups for every demographic—*TwilightMoms*, *Twilight Teens*, *Twilight Guy*, *Golden Twilighters*, and *TwiCrackAddict*—as well as fan communities from Spain to Romania to the United Arab Emirates. Brazil Twilighters are sponsoring a convention in 2011. Scattered around the fanpire are a few anti-Twilight websites, such as *Twilight Sucks*, which mock overzealous fans like the one who painstakingly painted Edward on her high-top sneakers. However, many of these had only a few hundred users, I found. After all, why spend hours online criticizing something you ostensibly detest?

At the zenith of the fanpire, wielding power judiciously and with relish are the *Twilight Lexicon*, *TwilightMoms*, *Twilight Guy*, *Twilighters*, *Twilight Series Theories*, *His Golden Eyes*, *BellaandEdward*, and others. They have reinvented themselves as Twilight power brokers. Summit Entertainment and other businesses eagerly court them to advertise the latest iPod application featuring Twilight and issue invitations to the chosen to visit film premieres and movie sets. One of the fan-site creators confided with me that the top fifteen websites have their own e-mail thread. "It's like our super secret e-mail thread, where we all talk about what's going on, and we pass along the news, and sometimes we have our own secret stuff that is like, 'Don't tell anyone this, but I heard this . . .'"

The fan sites' blessing or condemnation of a product can determine its ascendancy in the Twilight marketplace. They are the conduit through which the fanpire glimpses the glorious world of celebrity as well as the imaginary world of Twilight itself. You, too, may become famous, adored, sought-after, and a source of influence.

Lady Sybilla, a fan-fic writer, was one target of Alphie and Pel's censure and ire. In 2009, she published "Russet Noon," a sequel of sorts to *Breaking Dawn* in which Bella chooses Jacob instead of Edward. The book was popular among some readers, and Lady Sybilla attempted to publish it through her own company, AV Paranormal, and sell it on eBay. An uproar ensued over copyright issues after Lady Sybilla dared to link herself to the *Lexicon.* During an MTV interview, Alphie called "Russet Noon" the "story that must not be named." She posted explicitly about how the *Lexicon* doesn't endorse Lady Sybilla or her site, and that this situation illustrates why authors should not attempt to profit from fan fiction. One article dubbed Alphie and Pel "furies" and "Stephenie Meyer's wannabe watchdogs."[12]

The ingredients for potential fan celebrity consist of proximity to Stephenie Meyer; a blog, or, better yet, a vlog, or your own personal YouTube channel; a knack for self-promotion; and a transformative narrative of coming out as a celebrity. Those highest and most prominent in the hierarchy are those who can prove one degree of separation from Meyer, bestowing upon them cachet. When Meyer writes that she "laughed buckets" reading Kaleb Nation's *Twilight Guy,* it is the social capital of the fandom. Nation, whose posts about the series from a guy's perspective have catapulted him into the upper echelon of fan sites, lets it casually slip in our interview that he's especially close to Meyer, who now has no contact information anywhere on her website. "Every time I e-mail her, I'm like, I hope she's not too busy right now for me, because then, she's always doing so much, and I think, if I'm busy, she's got to be a billion times busier than I am . . ." he trails off. When Meyer changed her e-mail address, Nation recalled that "nobody knew where she was." He recounts the indignity of having to contact her publicist to explain, "I'm her friend. I need to talk to her."

Nation wrote *Bran Hambric and the Fairfield Curse,* a Harry Potteresque young adult novel about a boy with magical powers battling evil foes. He left college after a year to finish the book series and now has another book deal for a paranormal young adult series. His YouTube videos feature him at book signings, sitting in his living room, singing, or just being goofy, but when he interviewed Kristen Stewart at the *Twilight* premiere, his site garnered 1.5 million views, which bolsters his revenue. Another of the young fan-site creators (there are many in high school or just entering college) is Michelle Pan, an only child who runs *BellaandEdward*, which caters to readers between fifteen and twenty-six years old. Polite, on time, and impeccably dressed, she was accompanied to TwiCon by her parents. Although her site dates to the early days of 2006, and she's featured on panels and invited to film premieres, she lacks the swagger and even distracted air of some other fan celebs. Directing her giant website is wedged between doing homework, school band practice, and studying for SATs.

The moments when Kaleb Nation, Michelle Pan, or Lisa Hansen realized they were famous are cherished, expounded upon, and told and retold on their sites. Many such moments involve the opportunity to walk the red carpet at film premieres, not as true Twilight celebrities but as the engine behind the biggest fan sites. At the *Twilight* premiere, Pan witnessed throngs of screaming people and loud music blasting through speakers as she wandered lost around Mann's Chinese Theatre trying to find the press check-in. At a crosswalk, Pan was startled by a girl snapping her picture and told her, "Okay, I do not know who you are. That is a little creepy." According to Pan, the girl said, "You are Michelle from www.bellaandedward.com." "I said, 'Yeah, I am,' and she was like, 'Oh, my gosh, I visit your site a lot.'"

Kaleb Nation realized that the series had changed his life when he heard someone hollering his name at the *Twilight* film premiere. "I turned around and there was this crowd of people that were waving at me, trying to get me to go sign something. I was like, 'How do you know who I am?' They said, 'Well, we read your site.' And I just couldn't fathom the idea that someone that I didn't know knows who I am, and it was just amazing. I loved that." Caught up in this reverie, he asks me, "What was your original question?"

Female Fan Power?

Aside from Kaleb Nation of the *Twilight Guy* website and a few others, Twilight social media fan sites are staffed almost exclusively by women, who have garnered varying degrees of business acumen as a result of Twilight. Lisa Hansen of *TwilightMoms* is now a semifamous webmaster regularly interviewed by the media and is a featured speaker at Twilight conventions and events.

When I first met her at TwiCon, she was apologetic about her lateness and accompanied by her harried assistant, another Twilight mom. After joking with Larry Carroll, MTV's Twilight correspondent, we headed to the elevators where more fans accosted her for autographs. Her sense of her own celebrity was proudly emblazoned on the button she wore that read, "Yes, I am *the* Lisa." I'd told this story to another academic writing about Twilight, and we joked about donning similar buttons. Lisa admits that her husband admonishes her: "I told you to make a few friends. I did not tell you to build an empire." Her life as an LDS member and mother with a special-needs child also now features interviews with MTV and a personal assistant to cope with the deluge of fan e-mails. Lisa travels around the country, oversees the successful *TwilightMoms* movie events for the film premieres, and speaks to media regularly. All of these are opportunities she'd never have without Twilight.

At the San Francisco TwiTour, sisters Hanna and Hilly Hindi, or the Hillywood Players, are taking pictures with fans and signing autographs. I hear one girl call to another in awe, "It's the *Hillywood* people." With some of *The Hillywood Show*'s YouTube parodies garnering over 2 million views, it's not surprising that the women behind it are semifamous. They bound onto the stage to kick off the convention while they debut their latest *New Moon* spoof. *The Hillywood Show* straddles the line between fan-created media and striving celebrity wannabes. The Hindis, in their early twenties, write, produce, direct, and film the Twilight satires, which they post on YouTube and screen at events like the Summer School in Forks, TwiCon, and TwiTours.

In the tribute parodies, Hilly, pixiesh and petite with almost black eyes, is perfectly dressed as Bella. Hanna, the director who often doubles as Alice, is almost her twin, aside from her floppy bob haircut. They're generally accompanied by two friends who play the aloof and sulky versions of Edward and Jasper. As their bios read on their website, "The Hindi sisters are celebrities in their own right . . . but you wouldn't know it from talking to them. Extremely humble and grateful to the fans for their success (even in the midst of non-stop travel and endless autograph signings), Hilly and Hannah are a breath of fresh air in a fame-hungry world." They are funded entirely by the girls' personal incomes and rely on a single camera. On their website, the sisters plead, "One can only imagine what The Hillywood Show® could become with a full production studio at their fingertips."

Their elaborate *Twilight*, *New Moon*, and *Eclipse* parodies both ruthlessly mock and obsequiously honor the films, using fairly high production values and detailed costumes. The *Eclipse* parody begins with Bella and Edward discussing marriage. Then Bella bursts into Lady Gaga's song "Bad Romance," while she sexually attacks Edward, cavorts with the entire shirtless wolf pack at a club, and eventually shuns Edward by leaping into Jacob's arms at the vampire/werewolf treaty line when she sees Jacob's hefty pectoral muscles twitch. There is a hilarious send-up of the scene where the Cullens prepare for the newborn vampire army that is stalking them by practicing fight moves with each other. The Hillywood Players have them leap and hurtle themselves at each other spasmodically.

In another video, Hilly channels Bella in the scene after Edward tells her, "You don't belong in my world," and abandons her in the forest. Hilly (as Bella) lies in her bed in a depressive heap, mourning Edward. Suddenly she springs up and out from the covers dressed in skintight black leather pants and a black half-shirt while singing, "I'm a rock star. I don't want you." In the rest of the spoof, Bella chainsaws the tree where "Edward + Bella" was carved and flaunts a paw print with "Team Jacob" engraved on her lower back. Singing "Perfect little punching bag," from Pink's "Don't Leave Me," she runs back and forth between Edward and Jacob apologetically whining, "I'm sorry." The Hillywood performances are saucy, but never cross the line from irreverent to offensive or overtly critical because they're at the convention at the behest of Summit Entertainment. The videos provide fans with a jolt in the hiatus between films, a film about a film about a book, but the creators are also smart and savvy about promoting themselves at fan events. Twilight is a launch pad for potential film and acting careers. If they slog through the conventions and Stephenie Meyer Days now, they might be walking the red carpet themselves later.

Not all of the Twilight fan media is quite so carefully reverential, which is probably why Kiera Cass is not invited on the TwiTour circuit. Cass, a thirtysomething resident of Blacksburg, Virginia, is also part of the TwiCurls, the sister duo who ran "Cardio with the Cullens" at TwiCon. She posts videos about Twilight on their TwiCurls channel. Kiera has a modest audience of five thousand compared to *Hillywood*'s millions of hits, and she doesn't travel extensively because of her young child, but her caricatures of Twilight have a more subversive edge than *Hillywood*'s and are equally hilarious, if not more so.

On Valentine's Day, Kiera's YouTube video starts with her asking, "What could be more romantic than a valentine from Edward? On second thought . . ." She then gives us examples of Edward-inspired valentines: "My life is slightly less depressing now that you're in it." Or, "I know what color your toothbrush is even though you've never seen me. P.S. I'm a stalker." In another video, she flips through Photoshopped images of how the Cullens would have appeared in the 1980s. They always appear so classic, despite having been around hundreds of years, Kiera complains, so she's placed Carlisle and Esme posing in matching purple tracksuits. Of Edward and his hair, she says, "I have three words—Flock of Seagulls!"

Despite her upbeat personality, Kiera admits that her first book, *The Selection*, about a woman whose husband dies, was inspired by the horrific shootings on the Virginia Tech campus in 2007, when a gunman killed thirty-three people. Her husband was there that day. Like Meyer's tale of waking from a dream with the kernel of the Twilight book idea, Kiera's book came to her when she "just woke up from a nap with like four paragraphs, just the idea in my head. And it just sort of, kind of, kept me going. I had been writing other things before this, and it was mostly therapeutic, like just me dealing with fears." She now has a book deal for a paranormal series and shares an agent with Kaleb Nation.

The fan conventions are like networking occasions for more opportunities with the super-fans, who jockey to see who scores the interview and relish their shared fan fame. Lisa Hansen tells me that *TwilightMoms* extends beyond the computer into real life. "I have met Twilight moms from all over the world that have come who automatically know who I am and just want to say hi or take a picture. I feel like I have friends wherever I go. And that is just the richest blessing I could have ever gotten in my life."

Kaleb Nation, a former home-schooled kid from a small town in Texas, had never left his home state until the *Twilight* film premiere in California. Of that experience, he says, "That was a really big thing for me. I met so many people there. . . . That was the best of my life, that week there. So, I'm going to move to California. . . . Twilight has changed my everyday life, pretty much, more than almost anything else. The majority of the friends that I have now I met in the Twilight fandom, most of them at the *Twilight* premiere. I blog. I get to come to events like TwiCon. I go to all sorts of things that are related to Twilight, and if I had never gotten into the Twilight fandom, I wouldn't be doing any of that type of stuff. It's just a whole new part of my life now that I'm in the Twilight fandom."

Kaleb speaks of being part of a supportive community that has expanded his social world and connections: "I can go to an event, and if there are other people from other websites, even if I only know them online, it's like there's friends there." Kaleb met the *Lexicon*'s Alphie and Pel for the first time at the Summer School in Forks, and spent the long weekend driving around with them while they filmed themselves like high-spirited fans.

Kiera Cass's fan relationships blur the distinction between online and off. "It's like you get here and it's like, 'Oh, I haven't seen you in—Oh, I've never actually met you before!' and, like, it just doesn't feel that way because you've talked so many times." Cass calls the fans/friends "frans" when she meets them. When they tell her she's made their day, she responds, "And I'm like, 'Are you kidding!? That you wanna talk to me is making my day!'" Their catchphrase is the same: "It all began with Twilight, but now goes *so* much deeper." And this is the lure of the conventions, the online sites, the sales of the fangs and dildos: they offer affiliation, friends, recognition, or a way to make a living. The creators of these sites have built their identities and careers on Twilight, however precarious the edifice might be.

At the official TwiTour, Alphie and Pel perch on director chairs to commence one of the four talks they'll give that weekend. Alphie rhetorically asks the crowd if anyone read the series before January 2006, which was when she finished them. Without really waiting for an answer, Alphie continues, intending to establish her elder status in the fandom. "We find that most became fans because of their interest in the movies," she says. "But those of you that came into the fandom after the movies missed out on some of the most unique experiences the fandom had to offer."

Since many fans never get to visit Forks, Alphie and Pel's presentation about their driving tour of the reimagined Twilight setting and its environs is a surrogate experience. They are a bridge between the girl with the "stupid lamb" shirt and Stephenie Meyer, the film stars, and the insider scoop on Twilight. They can relay the glamour of the red carpet or the real Forks for the rest of us who never will get to interview Kellan Lutz.

Alphie and Pel both emphasize the fact they've been to Forks twice, recounting the prolonged drive, bumpy ferry ride, and towering forests. Pel tells us that though she's from New York and learned to drive in the Bronx, the winding roads past Crescent Lake to get to Forks were treacherous and harrowing. She jokes that fans should not speed because the state police particularly target Twilight fans for tickets. From their rehearsed banter and shtick, it's clear that Alphie and Pel have recounted their trips countless times. They regale us with stories of staying with the Quileutes in La Push, the reservation down the road from Forks where Jacob and the wolf pack reside; lounging around a bonfire; learning the differences between First, Second, and Third beaches; and listening to Chris Morganroth, a local man, convey Quileute legends. "I don't know what it all meant, but it was really intense," Alphie assures us.

She might have deferred to Anita Wheeler, a member of the tribe from La Push. Wheeler is a former teacher who has been telling her grandfather's stories for over thirty years. She gave talks at TwiCon but hasn't been invited on the official Creation TwiTours, where fans can indulge in their fascination with the tribe through Alphie and Pel's stories. While deeply frustrated by the abysmal level of knowledge many fans possess about Native Americans, Wheeler treats her talks as an opportunity to remedy the romanticization of the Quileutes, especially the idea that they can become wolves. "The fans believe what is written in the books and that is not who we are as people," she told me when I interviewed her at TwiCon. "We are nothing like that, and it is quite contrary to the traditional thought that I have been taught. So I think this turned this into something positive that I can live with, and so I have chosen to use it as a forum for me to relate to strangers who we are as people."

During their presentation, Alphie sprinkles her anecdotes with "you betcha," while Pel plays up the fast-talking East Coast stereotype. After the Forks spiel is over, they answer questions from the floor, or rather from the box in which fans have dropped them off: "Did you see wildlife?"; "Meet Stephenie Meyer?"; "Have you met Rob Pattinson!!?"

Pel regales us with how she filmed "Rob" at a premiere as another fan-site owner interviewed him. There are gasps from the audience. Of Meyer, Pel tells the crowd, "She's very generous to her fans, a very real person, and a gifted conversationalist. The first time we met her, we parked the car and thought, 'We'll just run downstairs and put money in the meter.' We actually got a parking ticket we were talking so long! That's just the kind of person she is, and I know not every author is like that. It can be risky sometimes, and a little frightening to be that exposed to your fans."

After their presentation, Alphie and Pel return to the Pendragon booth, where Pel tries on the dress she was eyeing earlier. I introduce myself and remind Alphie that I met her in Forks at the Summer School event. I'm curious to know what they can tell me about how the fandom has changed and the challenges of creating female-driven media. They've published thoughtful screeds against the anti-

Twilight bias of some journalists and pointed out that a lot of the criticism has to do with gender. I promise not to probe for personal details about Stephenie Meyer, and Alphie is guardedly friendly. She seems to be considering an interview, but Pel steps in and tells me emphatically that they won't answer questions, even general ones, about the fanpire for a book. It's as if behind every rejection and move lurk Hachette, Summit, and Creation, the giants that dare not be crossed. Then Pel buys the dress, and she and Alphie head back-stage to mingle with the other VIPs.

The Fog of Twilight

Gloomy, deserted streets dripping with rain greet me when I visit Forks in December 2011. Whereas there were close to 73,000 Twitourists in 2010, by the count at the Forks visitor center, only a little more than half that amount made the trek in 2011. As the countdown begins for *Breaking Dawn–Part 2*, the last film in the series, set to release in late 2012, the Twilight craze that drew thousands to this sleepy town may finally be dwindling. Forks could have another few years after the release of the final installment of *Breaking Dawn* until only the hardcore fans visit. Already there are signs that the boom period is over. Dazzled by Twilight, the largest Twilight store in town, is closing. The rumors and innuendo about the owner's business practices ran rampant: she overreached by emulating a Walmart model that squeezed out other vendors, didn't pay her taxes, hired "carnies" or unsavory transients who smoked outside her building and skimmed money off the till, or other merchants sabotaged her by writing to the state liquor board to deny her a license. This is the seedier side of the Twilight mania, one that tourists have never witnessed in a town that has had to adjust to a Wild West tourist rush that washed over them without warning.

The local pastor of a nondenominational church believes Forks has been in what he calls a "fog of Twilight." Although fans spend money at hotels, restaurants, and shops, most of the families at his church struggle as much as before, even though unlike other towns on the Olympic Peninsula, Forks's taxable retail sales have *increased* during the recession.[1] The pastor writes to me, "I'm bracing for the shock when the fog lifts, the movies are over, the books quit selling, and our poor community goes back to dealing with the reality of having to sustain itself economically." As if anticipating these concerns, Mike Gurling and Marcia Bingham at the Forks visitor center cling to the mantra I've heard from many residents: "We came because of Twilight; we'll be back because of Forks." They believe that the striking beauty of the area combined with the lingering aura of Twilight will entice people in the future. Members of the Stephenie Meyer Day committee have proposed to perform up to ten weddings per day during the three days leading up to August 13, the day Bella married Edward. They've promised that the wedding location will be an exact replica of the one in the film *Breaking Dawn–Part 1*, with flowered arches and wisteria. An ambitious plan to create a permanent Twilight museum to display all the collected paraphernalia in Forks is slated for a grand opening in 2014, though organizers haven't determined a location for it or found investors.[2]

The fans' loyalties are shifting to other books that are already blockbuster franchises, such as the popular *Hunger Games*, a trilogy by Suzanne Collins, with a love triangle and an intrepid teenage heroine who ignites a revolution in a totalitarian world. The much-anticipated movies are starting to emerge as I write. *TwilightMoms* is hosting a premiere party for the first Hunger Games film; the woman who writes the Twilight column for the *Twilight Examiner* is now penning a Hunger Games column on another site; and one fan site has reinvented itself to serve new fantasy films and media. Other fans are intrigued by Veronica Roth's *Divergent*, the first book in a trilogy set in a dystopian Chicago and featuring yet another dauntless young heroine.

The postapocalyptic worlds the young women in these books inhabit bear little resemblance to the romance-saturated Twilight saga. What is monstrous here is what humans do to each other. There is no need for vampires and werewolves. True love is a mere backdrop to other pressing questions: Am I courageous enough to speak up against injustice? Will I survive brutal physical and mental tests? Who do I love and trust? Do I remain true to myself or become part of a system I abhor? Although not explicitly feminist texts, *Hun-*

ger Games and *Divergent* address the core challenges that feminism poses about critiquing relations of power, imagining the world as other than it is, and envisioning alternative arrangements of work, life, and leisure for all of us. They are the kinds of questions I'd like my daughter and son to consider when they begin reading young adult literature.

❧

Susan of *Twilight Bond* occasionally blogs about the latest Bella and Edward wedding Barbie dolls, and she's purchased tickets for the Los Angeles Twilight convention to be held before the premiere of *Breaking Dawn–Part 2*. Bella's wedding dress was a huge hit after the movie, so the next coveted item for the fanpire may be Bella vampire contact lenses to mimic the change in her eyes as she morphs into a resplendent Amazonian vampire. Since conventions are geared to product tie-ins with the films, as well the chance for fans to get actors' autographs, their drawing power may subside with time. The fear is that after the last film there will only be a "crashing feeling of loss," as Susan confides to me over e-mail.

Nostalgia for the days of the peak fandom, when everything was new and the barrage of hype about the next book, movie, or casting choice fed a voracious appetite for all things Twilight, is already seeping into conversations on blogs and at conventions. At one blog, someone asked readers, "How will you keep the Twilight world alive?" Another person responded, "I almost cried reading ur post. 'Cuz really what will be left? I know nothing will go on forever and eventually we will all move on too, not to say we won't have a piece of it in our hearts forever and im sure as grandmothers our teenage grandchildren will stumble on to our books and we can open up a wonderful world to them. *Tears* & *sniffles*."

Others defiantly commented on this and other blogs that despite the bittersweet idea of the films ending, the phenomenon is only over when the fans say it is. The films and books may no longer be produced, but the world they evoke doesn't have to stop, one girl wrote. I imagine TwilightMoms will still have their sleepovers, and fans will still write more inventive and outlandish smut even as the well of inspiration dries up, and still forge their aberrant creations, like "Bella's womb," when rereading and rewatching aren't enough. The fanpire perhaps becomes a solitary place without the websites, conventions, blogs, and events to unite its members. Or, as at Star Trek conventions years after the TV series and films stopped being produced, fans will mingle with Edward and Bella impersonators at ten-year anniversaries of the books' publication, exchanging vintage Twilight merchandise and swapping old stories. A forty-year-old Robert Pattinson, his once uncontrollable hair now reduced to thinning baldness, his body inevitably collapsed into middle-age softness, can greet them as a special VIP guest.

"So, we grow up," a girl confesses in a YouTube video about the Twilight phenomenon, "but it will never be over as long as we remain loyal to the friendship, the hope, the power, the love, and the magic we found!" This may be bluster, a last stand against the inevitable end, or part of the eternal hope for more. The blogosphere is abuzz about *Twilight, the Musical* and with rumors of a *Twilight* television series. Thousands of fans will no doubt storm the theaters for *Breaking Dawn—Part 2*.

Imagine Better, a project initiated by Harry Potter fans, is attempting to rouse disparate fandoms, whether they slay or sparkle, into a united front to address issues relating to human rights, media, the environment, and other areas of concern. "All of our favorite movies, books and shows have heroes, villains, triumph and defeat. Every time we band together for good, we get exponentially stronger," reads the group's website. "One hero standing strong can change the world, so imagine what thousands of us together can do."

The Twilight fanpire as a rallying point for social change seems unlikely. Rather than a launching pad for revolution, Twilight is a soothing palliative of enchantment far from our own disappointing world of foreclosures, war, debt, and shriveled futures. It offers us, with the dazzling mirage of the meadow, the vampire, and the plain girl he worships, true love that lasts forever and the possibility of transforming our lives. The giddiness and joy overwhelms and propels the fanpire for a time. It consoles, buoys, and connects us, and then, like the fleeting sparkles on Edward's skin, it vanishes.

Acknowledgments

My temporary immersion in the fanpire of Twilight was sometimes bizarre but always fascinating. I owe my biggest debt to the women and men with whom I had formal and informal conversations at conventions and film premieres, and in workshops and on tours, and to the 594 people who responded to my online survey, many of whom later shared details of their lives in extended follow-up interviews. Their reflections on Twilight inform this book, even if they may not always agree with what I have written. I'm particularly grateful to the people of Forks and La Push, Washington, who took the time to speak with me on multiple occasions and offered their insights on vampire tourism: Marcia Bingham, Mike Gurling, Chris Cook, Kevin Rupprecht, Staci Chastain, Annette Root, Anita Wheeler, Rosemary Colandrea, and Charlene Cross. Thanks to the various fan-site creators and "twi-rock" musicians who generously agreed to interviews, especially Michelle Pan, Lisa Hansen, Twibond, Kiera Cass, Kaleb Nation, Chandler Nash, Ally Kiger, Tori Randall, Mitch Hansen, Brent Cook, Anita Wheeler, Megan Wilson, and Marie Martin.

I've benefited greatly from the expertise of colleagues and scholars who not only lent their formidable expertise on everything from girlhood to vampires, popular culture to religion, but who also shared with me the ambivalence of the fan and critic. This book is much better for the help and critical feedback of Mary Thomas, Rebecca Wanzo, Ananya Mukherjea, Amanda Rossie, Beth Shively, Natalie Wilson, Julie Sze, and Maggie Parke. Special thanks to Ann Neumann and Angela Zito at New York University's the *Revealer* and Carole Stabile at the University of Oregon's *Fembot* for publishing early versions of this book.

The Comparative Studies Department at Ohio State University has been an extremely supportive and collegial home for my work. Thank you especially to Julia Watson, Hugh Urban, and Gene Holland, as well as for the logistical support of Wen Tsai and Lori Wilson. At Ohio State, students in courses on popular culture, girlhood, religion, and media and in a seminar in the Honors and Scholars program were enthusiastic and challenging audiences who also perceptively discussed how Twilight resonates in their own lives.

At Beacon, Amy Caldwell's savvy editorial direction and discerning questions have vastly improved this book since its inception. Thanks, also, to Susan Lumenello for her copyediting acumen.

Baffled and bemused friends accompanied me to late-night film screenings, sent me a continual stream of zany Twilight-related material, and cheered me on. I'm immensely grateful for the friendship of Abby Crain, Mary Thomas, Shireen Deboo, Cathy Harris, Maisie Weissman, and Kim Gilmore.

Writing a book with two children under the age of four often feels like it requires supernatural intervention, and I often wished that, like the Cullen vampires, I didn't require sleep. For making the impossible balance somewhat tenable, I am fortunate to have my extended family: Alex Erzen; Angela Wallis; Annemarie, Jim, John, Tom, and James Quigley; Maria Riley; and George, Amy, Sandra, and David Marsh. Bob and Susan Erzen lent all manner of emotional and practical support, for which I am eternally grateful. Dazzling vampires pale before Bill Quigley, who sustained me through this process with patience, humor, and love. This book is dedicated to Matilda and Clive, who really do sparkle with delight and unbounded curiosity.

Notes

Quotes from the four Twilight series novels by Stephenie Meyer were taken from these editions: *Twilight* (2005), *New Moon* (2006), *Eclipse* (2007), and *Breaking Dawn* (2008), all published by Little, Brown.

INTRODUCTION. WELCOME TO THE TWILIGHT ZONE

1. Lev Grossman of *Time* coined the phrase "climb inside them and live there," which has been taken up by members of the fandom and is the name of a fan page on Facebook; I've also seen the phrase used on blogs.

2. BellaandEdward.com, a popular fan site, posted a link to my online survey from August to October of 2009. I had 594 responses to a set of 34 questions that included information on age, geographic location, sex, religion, occupation, relationship status, education level, and race, as well as the amount of time the respondent spent on Twilight-related activities, the kind of Twilight activities she engaged in, the kinds of events she attended, other kinds of books she read, and the number of times she had read the Twilight books and seen the films. Open-ended questions included how the respondent became a Twilight fan, why she read the series, her opinions about Bella and Edward's relationship, qualities she admired in the characters, qualities she didn't admire in the characters, and how the series had affected her relationships with friends, family, and significant others. Of these, 64.9 percent chose Bella and Edward's relationship as the one they would like to have; 67.5 percent also read romance fiction; 33 percent spent one to two hours per day on Twilight-related activities; and 51.5 percent said they believed in supernatural beings.

3. Fan studies emerged in 1992 with the publication of Henry Jenkins's *Textual Poachers: Television Fans and Participatory Culture* (New York: Routledge, 1992) and Camille Bacon-Smith's *Enterprising Women: Television Fandom and the Creation of Popular Myth* (Philadelphia: University of Pennsylvania Press, 1991). The study of fandoms is indebted to the earlier work of the Birmingham (UK) School of Cultural Studies. Other studies include Constance Penley's key essays on fans of "slash" (a genre of fan fiction that focuses on sex and romance

between characters of the same sex), such as "Feminism, Psychoanalysis, and Popular Culture," in *Cultural Studies,* Lawrence Grossberg et al., eds. (New York: Routledge, 1992), 479–500; and Lisa Lewis, *The Adoring Audience: Fan Culture and Popular Media* (New York: Routledge, 1992). Later scholars, such as Matt Hills, *Fan Cultures* (New York: Routledge, 2002), argued that the aforementioned books were too rationalized and insufficiently focused on issues of passion, desire, pleasure, and affect.

4. Henry Jenkins uses the term *nomadic* in *Textual Poachers: Television Fans and Participatory Culture* (New York: Routledge, 1992), and Jonathan Gray, Cornel Sandvoss, and C. Lee Harrington, eds., *Fandom: Identities and Communities in a Mediated World* (New York: New York University Press, 2007), also make this point, adding that attempting to classify audiences keeps us from understanding how they adapt to a text over time.

5. There has been some research on international fans, such as the Twilight Academy, a research group at Mid Sweden University's European Tourism Research Institute, which studies fan tourism and coined the term *twication.* The essay "Transnational Twilighters: A Twilight Fan Community in Norway," by Inger-Lise Kalviknes Bore and Rebecca Williams, in *Bitten by Twilight: Youth Culture, Media, and the Vampire Franchise,* Melissa Click et al., eds. (New York: Peter Lang, 2010), 189–204, is a study of Norwegian fans on online fan forums.

6. For abortion statistics in the United States, see the Guttmacher Institute, *Responsibility: Women, Society, and Abortion Worldwide* (New York: AGI, 1999); Susan Page, "Roe v. Wade: The Divided States of America," *USA Today,* April 17, 2006, http://www.usatoday.com/. For statistics on the prevalence of abstinence-only curricula, see Heather D. Boonstra, "Advocates Call for a New Approach after the Era of 'Abstinence-Only' Sex Education," *Guttmacher Policy Review* 12, no. 1 (Winter 2009), http://www.guttmacher.org/. For teen pregnancy rates, see "State Data," National Campaign to Prevent Teen and Unplanned Pregnancy, http://www.thenationalcampaign.org/.

7. For a robust discussion of the emergence of postfeminism through popular media in Britain and the United States, see Angela McRobbie, *The Aftermath of Feminism: Gender, Culture, and Social Change* (New York: Sage Publications, 2008); Susan Douglas, *Enlightened Sexism: The Seductive Message that Feminism's Work Is Done* (New York: Times Books, 2010); Diane Negra, *What a Girl Wants? Fantasizing the Reclamation of Self in Postfeminism* (New York: Routledge, 2008); Sarah Projansky, "Mass Magazine Cover Girls: Some Reflections on Postfeminist Girls and Postfeminism's Daughters," in *Interrogating Postfeminism: Gender and the Politics of Popular Culture,* Yvonne Tasker and Diane Negra, eds. (Durham, NC: Duke University Press, 2007), 40–72. Projansky argues that "the postfeminist subject is represented as having lost herself but then (re) achieving stability through romance, de-aging, a makeover, by giving up paid work, or by 'coming home.' . . . Popular culture insistently asserts that if women can

productively manage home, time, work, and their commodity choices, they will be rewarded with a more authentic, intact and achieved self." Peggy Orenstein writes about how specific modes of femininity and "girliness" are marketed in *Cinderella Ate My Daughter: Dispatches from the Front Lines of the New Girlie-Girl Culture* (New York: Harper, 2011).

8. Writing about adolescent girls who watched the short-lived television show *My So-Called Life*, Susan Murray argues that the girls understood the show as a parallel to their own lives and it helped them make sense of their identities; Susan Murray, "Saving Our So-Called Lives: Girl Fandom, Adolescent Subjectivity, and My So-Called Life," in *Dear Angela: Remembering My So-Called Life*, Michele Byers, ed. (Lanham, MD: Lexington Books, 2007).

9. Janice Radway's *Reading the Romance: Women, Patriarchy, and Popular Literature* (Chapel Hill: University of North Carolina Press, 1991) uses ethnography and interviews with romance readers to document their experiences as well as covering the economics of romance-fiction production. Despite her emphasis on the aesthetics of emotion and pleasure in romance reading, Radway still concludes that women's need for romance novels is "a function of their dependent status as women." She also argues that "romance reading originates in a very real dissatisfaction and embodies a valid if limited protest." In *Loving with a Vengeance: Mass-Produced Fantasies for Women*, 1st ed. (New York: Routledge, 1982), Tania Modleski writes about Harlequin novels from the late 1970s, as well as gothic novels and television soap operas, but she uses psychoanalysis to examine the way women read them. Modleski argues that the selfless "disappearing act" seemingly required of both heroine and reader has beneath it an outlet for feminine (if not feminist) rage. Another, more recent ethnography of working-class high school students reading romance fiction is Carol Ricker-Wilson, "Busting Textual Bodices: Gender, Reading, and the Popular Romance Author(s)," *English Journal* 88, no. 3 (January 1999), 57- 64.

10. Pamela Regis, *A Natural History of the Romance Novel* (Philadelphia: University of Pennsylvania Press, 2003).

11. Irin Carmon, "Romance Novels Are Steaming Up E-Reader Screens," *Fast Company* June 22, 2011, http://www.fastcompany.com/, accessed September 21, 2011.

12. In *Seduced by Twilight: The Allure and Contradictory Messages of the Popular Saga* (Jefferson, NC: McFarland, 2011), Natalie Wilson provides the first sustained feminist textual analysis of the Twilight series.

13. Edited collections about Twilight include Giselle Liza Anatol, ed., *Bringing Light to Twilight: Perspectives on a Pop Culture Phenomenon* (New York: Palgrave MacMillan, 2011); Rebecca Housel and J. Jeremy Wisnewski, eds., *Twilight and Philosophy: Vampires, Vegetarians, and the Pursuit of Immortality* (New Jersey: John Wiley, 2009); Nancy Reagin, ed., *Twilight and History*, 1st ed. (New Jersey: John Wiley, 2010); Click et al., eds., *Bitten by Twilight*; Maggie

Parke and Natalie Wilson, eds., *Theorizing Twilight: Critical Essays on What's at Stake in a Post-Vampire World* (Jefferson, NC: McFarland, 2011). The film *Vampires Suck* is a notable satire of *Twilight*, as is the Harvard Lampoon's *Nightlight: A Parody* (New York: Vintage, 2009), in which "Edwart Mullen" is the vampire. The book bills itself as "complete with romance, danger, insufficient parental guardianship, creepy stalkerlike behavior and a vampire prom." Brian Leaf's *Defining Twilight: Vocabulary Workbook for Unlocking the SAT, ACT, GED, and SSAT* (New Jersey: John Wiley, 2009) is a clever use of Twilight vocabulary for fans who must study for standardized tests; subsequent vocabulary books have been published following each new volume in the Twilight series.

14. Elaine A. Heath makes this apt point in *The Gospel According to Twilight: Women, Sex, and God* (Louisville, KY: Westminster John Knox Press, 2011).

15. Jen Yamato, "Top Ten *New Moon* Facts Revealed at Comic-Con," *Rotten Tomatoes*, July 27, 2009, *www.rottentomatoes.com/*

16. Ibid.

17. Gray, Sandvoss, and Harrington in *Fandom* also critique the belittling of fans in general and the way it "reveals a firm desire to understand fandom solely as Other."

18. See Hills, *Fan Cultures.*

19. I borrow this idea from Slavoj Zizek, who writes, "We mistake for postponement of the 'thing itself' what is already the 'thing itself,' we mistake for the searching and indecision proper to desire what is, in fact, the realization of desire. That is to say, the realization of desire does not consist in its being 'fulfilled,' 'fully satisfied,' it coincides rather with the reproduction of desire as such, with its circular movement." Slavoj Zizek, *Looking Awry: An Introduction to Jacques Lacan through Popular Culture* (Cambridge, MA: MIT Press, 1992), 7.

CHAPTER 1. I'M IN LOVE WITH A FICTIONAL CHARACTER

1. Marnina Gonick, "Between 'Girl Power' and 'Reviving Ophelia': Constituting the Neoliberal Girl Subject," *National Women's Studies Association Journal* 18, no. 2 (2006): 1–23.

2. Angela McRobbie, "Top Girls: Young Women and the Post-Feminist Sexual Contract," *Cultural Studies* 21, nos. 4–5 (July/September 2007): 718–37.

3. Angela McRobbie, "Post-Feminism and Popular Culture," *Feminist Media Studies* 4, no. 3 (2004): 261.

4. Angela McRobbie, *The Aftermath of Feminism: Gender, Culture and Social Change* (Thousand Oaks, CA: Sage, 2009).

5. The broader academic discussion of the issue of choice and the constraints of girlhood as an experience and an identity is varied. See Marnina Gonick, *Between Femininities: Ambivalence, Identity, and the Education of Girls* (Albany: State University of New York Press, 2003); Anita Harris, *Future Girl: Young*

Women in the Twenty-first Century (New York: Routledge, 2004); Valerie Hey, "The Girl in the Mirror: The Psychic Economy of Class in the Discourse of Girlhood Studies," *Girlhood Studies* 2, no. 2 (2009):10–32; Valerie Walkerdine et al., *Growing Up Girl: Psychosocial Explorations of Gender and Class* (New York: New York University Press, 2001); Mary E. Thomas, "Resisting Mothers, Making Gender: Teenage Girls in the United States and the Articulation of Femininity," *Gender, Place and Culture* 15, no. 1 (February 2008): 61–74; Mary E. Thomas, *Multicultural Girlhood: Racism, Sexuality and the Conflicted Spaces of American Education* (Philadelphia: Temple University Press, 2011).

6. Jana Riess, "Mormon Women, Twilight, and Internalized Sexism," *Beliefnet*, June 6, 2011, http://blog.beliefnet.com/.

7. The most well-known of the popular paranormal romance genre is Charlaine Harris's Southern Vampire Mysteries, which feature Sookie Stackhouse and were transformed into the HBO series *True Blood*. Other similar series include J. R. Ward's Black Dagger Brotherhood, Kresley Cole's Immortals After Dark, Lara Adrian's Midnight Breed, Laurell K. Hamilton's Anita Blake, and Sherrilyn Kenyon's Dark-Hunter.

8. For examples of this argument, see Richard Bogg and Janet M. Ray, "Byronic Heroes in American Popular Culture: Might They Adversely Affect Mate Choice?" *Deviant Behavior: An Interdisciplinary Journal* 23 (2002): 203–33; Christine M. Bachen and Eva Illouz, "Imagining Romance: Young People's Cultural Models of Romance and Love," *Critical Studies in Mass Communication* 13, no. 4 (December 1996); Bjarne M. Holmes and Kimberly R. Johnson, "Where Fantasy Meets Reality: Media Exposure, Relationship Beliefs and Standards, and the Moderating Effect of a Current Relationship," in *Social Psychology: New Research*, Ellen P. Lamont, ed. (Hauppauge, NY: Nova Science Publishers, 2009).

9. Pamela Regis, *A Natural History of the Romance Novel* (Philadelphia: University of Pennsylvania Press (2003).

CHAPTER 2. SPARKLE, YOU FOOL, SPARKLE!

1. Byron Beck, "Mommie Fiercest: Portland Invaded by Vampires . . . and 'Stalker' Moms?" *Willamette (OR) Week* online, April 30, 2008, http://www.wweek.com/.

2. Jeff Gordinier, "So the Woman You Love Has the Hots for a Vampire. What Does That Say about You?" *Details*, November 17, 2009.

3. Stephanie Coontz, *Marriage, A History: How Love Conquered Marriage* (New York: Penguin, 2008).

4. For an analysis of the wedding-industrial complex and the selling of the American wedding, see Rebecca Mead, *One Perfect Day: The Selling of the American Wedding* (New York: Penguin, 2008).

5. In her interviews with Twilight fans in two urban areas, Ananya Mukher-

jea found that one gay male fan's sexuality was openly discussed for the first time with relatives in a debate over Team Edward versus Team Jacob, which led to an unexpected acceptance. Ananya Mukherjea, "Team Bella: Twilight Fans Navigating Desire, Security, and Feminism," in *Theorizing Twilight: Critical Essays on What's at Stake in a Post-Vampire World*, in Maggie Parke and Natalie Wilson, eds. (Jefferson, NC: McFarland, 2011).

6. Melissa Click, "Twilight Follows Tradition: Analyzing 'Biting' Critiques of Vampire Narratives for their Portrayals of Gender and Sexuality," *Bitten by Twilight: Youth Culture, Media, and the Vampire Franchise*, Melissa Click et al., eds. (New York: Peter Lang, 2010), p. 138.

7. Trace Lamb, "Twilighting: Wanna Know What Women Want?" *Sunstone: Mormon Experience, Scholarship, Issues and Art* (December 2008): 38–39.

8. Christine Spines, "When 'Twilight' Fandom Becomes Addiction: Some Fans of the Book and Film Series Are Finding Their Obsession Is Hurting Other Parts of Their Lives," *Los Angeles Times*, June 27, 2010.

9. Hanna Rosin, "The End of Men," *Atlantic*, July/August 2010; Liza Mundy, *The Richer Sex: How the New Majority of Female Breadwinners Is Transforming Sex, Love, and Family* (New York: Simon and Schuster, 2012).

10. Ann Friedman, "Beyond Hillary: Strength in Numbers," *American Prospect*, June 19, 2008.

11. "No News Is Bad News: Women's Leadership Still Stalled in Corporate America," press release, Catalyst, December 14, 2011, http://catalyst.org/, accessed January 1, 2012.

12. Kathleen Gerson, *The Unfinished Revolution: How a New Generation Is Reshaping Family, Work, and Gender in America* (New York: Oxford University Press, 2009); Ann Friedman, "Not Everything Has Changed: The Women's Movement May Have Changed Everything for the American Public, but in the Home, the Revolution Has Hardly Begun," *American Prospect*, December 20, 2009.

13. Irin Carmon, "Women's Progress Marches Backward," *Salon*, December 19, 2011, http://www.salon.com/.

14. Susan Douglas, *The Rise of Enlightened Sexism: How Pop Culture Took Us from Girl Power to Girls Gone Wild* (New York: St. Martin's Griffin, 2010).

CHAPTER 3. FAMILIES THAT PREY TOGETHER, STAY TOGETHER

1. Elaine A. Heath, *The Gospel According to Twilight: Women, Sex, and God* (Louisville, KY: Westminster John Knox Press, 2011). Another article that historicizes the notion of the Cullens as the ideal family is Kyra Glass von der Osten, "Like Other American Families, Only Not: The Cullens and the Ideal Family in American History," *Twilight and History*, Wiley Pop Culture and History Series, Nancy Reagin, ed. (Hoboken, NJ: John Wiley, 2010).

2. Heath, *The Gospel According to Twilight*, 11.

3. An excellent examination of the stereotypes attached to the Quileutes can be found on the webpage "Truth versus Twilight," created by the Burke Museum of Natural History and Culture at the University of Washington, http://www.burkemuseum.org/. Natalie Wilson also describes the racism of the Twilight series in her article "Civilized Vampires versus Savage Werewolves," in *Bitten by Twilight: Youth Culture, Media, and the Vampire Franchise*, Melissa Click et al., eds. (New York: Peter Lang, 2010).

4. Maxine Hanks, "Do Mormons Dream of Monstrous Gods? Stephenie Meyer's Twilight Myth as Mormon Heroine's Journey," *Sunstone: Mormon Experience, Scholarship, Issues and Art*, December 2009, p. 26.

5. See, for example, Marc E. Shaw, "For the Strength of Bella? Meyer, Vampires, and Mormonism," *Twilight and Philosophy: Vampires, Vegetarians, and the Pursuit of Immortality*, Rebecca Housel and J. Jeremy Wisnewski, eds. (Hoboken, NJ: John Wiley, 2009), 227–36; Edwin B. Arnaudin, "Mormon Vampires: The Twilight Saga and Religious Literacy," master's thesis, University of North Carolina at Chapel Hill, 2008; Anthony Petro and Samira K. Mehta, "Big Vampire Love: What's So Mormon about *Twilight?*" *Religion Dispatches*, December 4, 2009, http://www.religiondispatches.org/.

6. H. Davis Farnsworth, "Vampire Families Are Forever," *Sunstone: Mormon Experience, Scholarship, Issues and Art*, December 2009, 31.

7. Richard N. Ostling and Joan K. Ostling, *Mormon America: The Power and the Promise* (New York: HarperCollins, 1999), 165.

8. Ibid., 190.

9. Farnsworth, "Vampire Families Are Forever," 37.

10. Amanda Bell, "Twilight Series Spawns Religion: Edward Cullen Is Real, Members Should Read the Books Like a Bible," "Twilight Examiner" column, Examiner.com, April 2, 2009, http://www.examiner.com/.

11. Ibid.

12. Comparing fandom to religion has been discussed within the field of fan studies, including in a study that used surveys to determine if secular and religious fans responded differently to various questions. However, this study takes the terms "secular" and "religious" to be distinctly different and self-evident. Stephen Reysen, "Secular versus Religious Fans: Are They Different? An Empirical Study," *Journal of Religion and Popular Culture* 12 (Spring 2006).

13. Christopher Partridge, *Re-Enchantment of the West: Alternative Spiritualities, Sacralization, Popular Culture, and Occulture* (London: T&T Clark, 2005).

14. Robert D. Putnam and David E. Campbell, "Walking Away from Church," *Los Angeles Times*, October 17, 2010.

15. Lillian Daniel, "Spiritual but Not Religious? Please Stop Boring Me," *Washington Post*, August 31, 2011.

16. Gary Laderman, *Sacred Matters: Celebrity Worship, Sexual Ecstasies, the Living Dead, and Other Signs of Religious Life in the United States* (New York: New Press, 2010), 16.

17. John Granger, *Spotlight: A Close-Up Look at the Artistry and Meaning of the Twilight Novels* (Cheshire, CT: Zossima Press, 2010).

18. Stacey Lingle, "What Shines in *Twilight*? Looking at Four Key Ideas of the Vampire Saga That Stand Out for Christ Followers," *Christianity Today*, October 2, 2008.

19. Beth Felker Jones, *Touched by a Vampire: Discovering the Hidden Messages in the Twilight Saga* (Colorado Springs, CO: Multnomah Books, 2009), 161.

20. Ibid., 169.

21. Heath, *The Gospel According to Twilight*.

22. Steve Wohlberg, *The Trouble with Twilight: Why Today's Vampire Craze Is Hazardous to Your Health* (Shippensburg, PA: Destiny Image, 2010).

23. Julianne Escobedo Shepherd, "10 Pop Monstrosities That Almost Destroyed Our Culture in 2011," *Alternet*, December 30, 2011, http://www.alternet.org/.

24. Paul Elie, *The Life You Save May Be Your Own: An American Pilgrimage* (New York: Farrar, Straus and Giroux, 2004).

25. I write about this at more length in Tanya Erzen, "The Vampire Capital of the World: Enchantment and Commerce in Forks, WA," in *Theorizing Twilight: Critical Essays on What's at Stake in a Post-Vampire World*, Maggie Parke and Natalie Wilson, eds. (Jefferson, NC: McFarland Press, 2011).

26. Jana Riess, "Book of Mormon Stories That Steph Meyer Tells to Me: LDS Themes in the Twilight Saga and *The Host*," *BYU Studies Journal* 48, no. 3 (2009), https://byustudies.byu.edu/.

27. Media scholars like Lynn Schofield Clark have insightfully analyzed how teenagers define spirituality and religion in relation to popular media. See Lynn Schofield Clark, "U.S. Adolescent Religious Identity, the Media, and the 'Funky' Side of Religion," *Journal of Communication* 52, no. 4 (2002): 794–812; and Lynn Schofield Clark, *From Angels to Aliens: Teenagers, the Media, and the Supernatural* (New York: Oxford University Press, 2003).

28. Hanks, "Do Mormons Dream of Monstrous Gods?"; Ken Conger, "Did You Miss the Buzz? Teen Wolves Descend Upon San Antonio High Schools," KENS5-San Antonio, May 17, 2010, http://www.kens5.com/, accessed January 23, 2012.

29. Brian Chasnoff, "Teens' Lives Were Troubled," *My San Antonio*, October 1, 2010, http://www.mysanantonio.com/, accessed February 24, 2012.

CHAPTER 4. THE FORBIDDEN FRUIT TASTES THE SWEETEST

1. Lev Grossman, "Stephenie Meyer: A New J.K. Rowling?" *Time*, April 24, 2008.

2. Christine Seifert, "Bite Me! (Or Don't)," *Bitch*, December 16, 2008.

3. Julie Parrish, "Back to the Woods: Narrative Revisions in New Moon Fan Fiction at Twilighted.net," in *Bitten by Twilight: Youth Culture, Media, and the Vampire Franchise*, Melissa Click et al., eds. (New York: Peter Lang, 2010).

4. Jenkins wrote about how fan fiction became a recognizable form in the 1960s and 1970s in fanzines that circulated at science fiction conventions and by mail order, but this world has changed with the Internet. The Star Trek franchise has long been an object of study, but it generates a tenth of the fan fiction that Twilight or Harry Potter does. Henry Jenkins, *Textual Poachers: Television Fans and Participatory Culture* (New York: Routledge, 1992), 177. See also, Rebecca W. Black, *Adolescents and Online Fan Fiction* (New York: Peter Lang, 2008).

5. Romance Writers of America, *2005 Market Research Study on Romance Readers*. Complete report available at http://www.rwa.org/.

6. Sarah Wendell and Candy Tan, *Beyond Heaving Bosoms: The Smart Bitches' Guide to Romance Novels* (New York: Simon and Schuster, 2009).

7. True Love Waits was founded in 1993 by Southern Baptist youth minister Richard Ross as a Christian sex-education program with the sole purpose of promoting premarital sexual abstinence. The hallmarks of TLW are its public displays of signed pledge cards; in 2004, the group displayed over 460,000 cards from twenty different countries during the 2004 Summer Olympics in Athens. The Silver Ring Thing also emerged in the mid-1990s through the efforts of youth ministers Denny and Amy Pattyn, who wanted to emphasize Christian faith as a central part of abstinence; the program was federally funded in 2003 through the Maternal and Child Health Special Programs of Regional and National Significance Block Grant. For more on the history of the abstinence movement, see Sara Moslener, "Saving Civilization: Sexual Purity from the White Cross to the Silver Ring" (unpublished manuscript, 2012).

8. For critiques of abstinence-only curricula and the premise of abstinence education, see Jessica Fields and Celeste Hirschman, "Citizenship Lessons in Abstinence-Only Sexuality Education," *American Journal of Sexuality Education* 2, no. 2 (2007): 3–25; Jessica Fields and Deborah L. Tolman, "Risky Business: Sexuality Education and Research in U.S. Schools," *Sexuality Research and Social Policy* 3, no. 4 (2006): 63–76; Jessica Fields, *Risky Lessons: Sex Education and Social Inequality* (New Brunswick, NJ: Rutgers University Press, 2008); Janice Irvine, *Talk About Sex: The Battles over Sex Education in the United States* (Berkeley: University of California Press, 2002).

9. US House of Representatives Committee on Government Reform, Minority Staff Special Investigations Division, "The Content of Federally Funded Abstinence-Only Education Programs," prepared for Rep. Henry A Waxman, American Public Health Association, December 2004, www.apha.org/. See also, Martha E. Kempner, *Toward a Sexually Healthy America: Abstinence-Only-Until-Marriage Programs That Try to Keep Our Youth "Scared Chaste"* (New York: Sexuality Information and Education Council, 2001), 46–47.

10. Peter S. Bearman and Hannah Bruckner, "Promising the Future: Virginity Pledges as They Affect Transition to First Intercourse," Institute for Social and Economic Theory and Research, July 15, 2000; Hannah Bruckner with Peter S. Bearman, "After the Promise: The STD Consequences of Adolescent Virginity Pledges," *Journal of Adolescent Health* 36 (2005): 271–78.

11. Dagmar Herzog, *Sex in Crisis: The New Sexual Revolution and the Future of American Politics* (New York: Basic Books, 2008), 99.

12. Christine Gardner, *Making Chastity Sexy: The Rhetoric of Evangelical Abstinence Campaigns* (Berkeley: University of California Press, 2011).

13. Belinda Luscombe, "Well, Hello, Suckers," *Time*, February 19, 2006.

14. Donna Freitas, "The Next Dead Thing," *Publishers Weekly*, November 17, 2008.

15. Wendell and Tan, *Beyond Heaving Bosoms*, 45.

16. Ibid., 87.

17. Donna Freitas, *Sex and the Soul: Juggling Sexuality, Spirituality, Romance, and Religion on America's College Campuses* (New York: Oxford University Press, 2008).

18. See Pamela Paul, *Pornified: How Pornography Is Transforming Our Lives, Our Relationships, and Our Families* (New York: Times Books, 2005), for a discussion of how pornography has affected what men expect from women in the bedroom.

19. Peggy C. Giordano et al., "Gender and the Meanings of Adolescent Romantic Relationships: A Focus on Boys," *American Sociological Review* 71, no. 2 (April 2006): 260–87. Their findings suggest that adolescent boys are "more emotionally engaged in romantic relationships than previous characterizations would lead us to expect."

20. For scholarly assessment of this paradigm, see Emma Charlton, "'Bad' Girls versus 'Good' Girls: Contradiction in the Constitution of Contemporary Girlhood," *Discourse: Studies in the Cultural Politics of Education* 28, no. 1 (2007): 121–31; Meda Chesney-Lind and Katherine Irwin, "From Badness to Meanness: Popular Constructions of Contemporary Girlhood," in *All about the Girl: Culture, Power, and Identity*, Anita Harris, ed. (New York: Routledge, 2004).

21. Amy C. Wilkins, *Wannabes, Goths, and Christians: The Boundaries of Sex, Style, and Status* (Chicago: University of Chicago Press, 2008).

22. For a complicated reading of the limitations of girls' sexual choices and the way sexuality can empower girls, see Sharon Thompson, *Going All the Way: Teenage Girls' Tales of Sex, Romance, and Pregnancy* (New York: Hill and Wang, 1995); Karin A. Martin, *Puberty, Sexuality, and the Self: Girls and Boys at Adolescence* (New York: Routledge, 1996); Deborah L. Tolman, *Dilemmas of Desire: Teenage Girls Talk about Sexuality* (Cambridge, MA: Harvard University Press, 2002); Laura M. Carpenter, *Virginity Lost: An Intimate Portrait of First Sexual Experiences* (New York: New York University Press, 2005); Amy Schalet, "Sub-

jectivity, Intimacy, and the Empowerment Paradigm of Adolescent Sexuality: The Unexplored Room," *Feminist Studies* 35, no. 1 (2009).

23. Jenny Anderson, "National Study Finds Widespread Sexual Harassment of Students in Grades 7 to 12," *New York Times*, November 11, 2011.

24. Thompson, *Going All the Way*, 22.

25. Freitas, *Sex and the Soul*, 106.

26. Wendell and Tan, *Beyond Heaving Bosoms*.

27. Ken Gelder writes that vampires have historically represented anxieties and crises around colonization or reverse colonialism from the British perspective. He argues that anti-Semitism against eastern European Jews was folded into what became the Dracula myth. Vampires have also stood for anti-capitalism in which Capital is dead labor, which, vampire-like, lives only by sucking living labor. Ken Gelder, *Reading the Vampire* (Oxford, UK: Taylor and Francis, 2002). For the history of representations of the vampire, see Matthew Beresford, *From Demons to Dracula: The Creation of the Modern Vampire Myth* (London: Reaktion Books, 2005).

28. Sue-Ellen Case, "Tracking the Vampire," *Differences: A Journal of Feminist Cultural Studies* 3, no. 2 (1991): 3: "The structural importance of what is designated as unspeakable in this fiction: one knows what the unspeakable is precisely because it has no name. . . . In vampire fiction, vampirism becomes the means of animating the unspeakable, of bringing it to life. We can at least say that Lord Ruthven is a vampire—and this is because we cannot say that he is gay."

29. Ananya Mukherjea, "My Vampire Boyfriend: Postfeminism and 'Perfect' Masculinity," *Studies in Popular Culture* 33, no. 2 (Spring 2011).

30. Lisa LaPlante and Smita Kalokhe, "Police Say Man Did Not Bite Teen After Watching 'The Twilight Saga: New Moon'" *FOX 17 News Reporter*, November 25, 2009, http://www.fox17online.com/, accessed February 28, 2012.

CHAPTER 5. WHERE TO SPEND THOSE TWILIGHT DOLLARS

1. Author's e-mail correspondence with Laura Cristiano (Pel), June 1, 2011.

2. "Summit Entertainment and Creation Entertainment to Produce the Official TWILIGHT Fan Conventions," press release, Los Angeles, August 17, 2009, http://twilightconvention.com/, accessed February 28, 2012.

3. *From Participatory Culture to Public Participation*, a blog created by Henry Jenkins and students at the University of Southern California, http://sites .google.com/site/participatorydemocracyproject/.

4. B. Howell Belser, "Imagine Better: Can Harry Potter Change the World?" *Religion Dispatches*, November 26, 2010.

5. LeakyCon, http://www.leakycon.com/, accessed June 8, 2011.

6. *From Participatory Culture to Public Participation*.

7. Matt Hills, *Fan Cultures* (New York: Routledge, 2002).

8. Marianne Martens, "Consumed by Twilight: The Commodification of Young Adult Literature," in *Bitten by Twilight: Youth Culture, Media, and the Vampire Franchise*, Melissa Click et al., eds. (New York: Peter Lang, 2010), 243.

9. Nara Schoenberg, "Baby Names with Some Bite: 'Twilight'-Inspired Baby Names Have Supernatural Appeal," *Chicago Tribune*, July 27, 2010.

10. "Robert Pattinson's Sperm Can Be Yours," *MomLogic*, August 17, 2009, http://www.momlogic.com/.

11. Larissa Faw, "Tween Sensibility, Spending and Influence," EPM Communications, September 2010. See also, Claudia Mitchell and Jacqueline Reid-Walsh, *Seven Going On Seventeen: Tween Studies in the Culture of Girlhood* (New York: Peter Lang, 2005).

12. "Twilight Lexicon's Lori Joffs Refers to Russet Noon as 'The Story That Must Not Be Named' on MTV," EIN Presswire, http://www.einpresswire.com/; "Whose Characters Are They Anyway?" *Twilight Lexicon*, April 8, 2009, http://www.twilightlexicon.com/.

AFTERWORD

1. George Erb, "How 'Twilight' Juiced Forks' Economy," *Puget Sound (Seattle) Business Journal*, June 28, 2010.

2. Arwyn Rice and Leah Leach, "Twilight of an Era? Or a New Dawn?" *Peninsula Daily (WA) News*, February 19, 2012.

Index

3 3132 03394 8847
OKANAGAN PUBLIC LIBRARY